Environmental Ethics and Christian Humanism

Abingdon Press Studies in Christian Ethics and Economic Life

ABINGDON PRESS STUDIES IN CHRISTIAN ETHICS
AND ECONOMIC LIFE, VOLUME 2

Environmental Ethics and Christian Humanism

Thomas Sieger Derr

With Critical Responses by
James A. Nash
and
Richard John Neuhaus

Introduction by
Max L. Stackhouse

Abingdon Press
Nashville

ENVIRONMENTAL ETHICS AND CHRISTIAN HUMANISM

Library of Congress Cataloging-in-Publication Data

Derr, Thomas Sieger, 1931–
    Environmental ethics and Christian humanism / Thomas Sieger Derr;
with critical responses by James A. Nash and Richard John Neuhaus;
introduction by Max L. Stackhouse.
       p.   cm. — (Abingdon Press studies in Christian ethics and economic
life; vol. 2)
    Includes bibliographic references.
    ISBN 0-687-00161-7 (alk. paper)
    1. Human ecology—Religious aspects—Christianity. 2. Environmental
ethics. I. Nash, James A., 1938–   . II. Neuhaus, Richard John. III. Title.
IV. Series: Abingdon Press studies in Christian ethics and economic life: #2.
BT695.5.D38   1966
241´.691—dc20   96-43923
                                                 CIP

Parts of chapters 1 and 2 originally appeared in Michael J. Cromartie (ed.), *Creation at Risk? Religion, Science, and Environmentalism*, copyright © 1995 by William B. Eerdmans Publishing Company, and are here used by permission.

Parts of the section "The Animal Rights Distraction" of chapter 1 were first published in the journal *First Things* 18 (Feb. 1992), and are here used by permission.

Contents

Preface

This series is written to aid in the reconstruction of Christian ethics as it bears on economic life in our increasingly global era. Reconstruction is necessary because much of the analysis used by theologians and pastors to think about economic life in the past few decades is socially and theologically suspect.

It is not only political scientists who failed to predict the collapse of Eastern Europe by failing to read the signs of the times. Nor was it only economists who argued for massive loans by private banks to doubtful governments and did not foresee the consequences of these debts. Nor can we say it was only sociologists who denied the evidence of religious resurgence around the world because they believed that modernization would secularize everyone, or only anthropologists who argued that religion is an aspect of culture and every culture's ethic is equal to every other one, or only politicians who began to see all issues only in terms of power analysis. It was not even only philosophers and literary critics who began to deconstruct every normative claim. These all contributed to the demoralization of intellectual and religious life, to a vacuity in social ethics; but, it must be said, so also did the theologians and pastors.

In conferences on the implications of the Fall of the Wall sponsored by the Lilly Endowment, one hosted by Trotz Rendtorff in Munich and the other by Peter Berger in Boston, it became obvious that ideological commitments had obscured for many the deeper social and ethical forces, as well as many biblical and theological motifs, over the past several decades. It is not that no contribution to the future was made in these decades. Some evil was undone; some good was done. Many colonial, racist, and sexist structures were challenged if not fully banished, and many people were exposed to new possibilities. But many views of what brought these about, and many of the theologies and social theories which advocates use to guide the present toward the future are thin, false, confused, or

7

perilous. They cannot help us discover the ethical fabric for a global society.

We are closer to Ezra and Nehemiah, rebuilding the city on the base of the past, or the early church, engaging and reshaping a cosmopolitan culture, than we are to the Exodus, the Conquest, the Apocalypse, or the New Jerusalem. The prophetic task today is boldly to reconstruct social ethics under insecure and ambiguous conditions, while confessing our sins and seeking to be socially realistic, intellectually cogent, and theologically faithful.

To reform ethics, we offer a series of volumes, exploring the following hypotheses, recognizing that not everyone agrees:

- We face the prospect of a worldwide, multicultural society in which democratic, constitutional polities, human rights, ethnic interests, nationalist forces, media images, and corporate capitalist forces will be influential—and in conflict, needing ethical guidance.

- Economic forces are largely driving these developments and are themselves substantially driven by materialistic motivations, but they are also shaped by and subject to social, cultural, and spiritual influences, even if these are presently confused, inarticulate, or questionable.

- Religion invariably shapes a society's cultural and spiritual values; thus, no area of social life is purely secular, but since religion exists in the midst of social realities, it makes a great deal of difference what religion is present and how it relates to social realities.

- Economic life, as a peculiar mix of calculated interest, social-political formation, and religio-ethical commitment, stands as a key test as to whether the future will be a blessing or a curse to humanity.

- Theological understandings of the Bible and the classic tradition, in a reconstructive dialogue with the social and human sciences, can correct religious errors, contribute to the understanding of social and economic life, and render a Christian ethic to guide the emerging world civilization.

Such issues will be pursued by the method of "apologetic dialogue." "Apologetics" is often contrasted to "dogmatics," which seeks to set forth the doctrinal teaching of the church on its own terms. Dogmatics has its important place, and will often serve as a resource to our efforts. But apologetics seeks to show when, where, and how Christian faith and ethics are intellectually and morally valid and to engage in critical and mutually corrective dialogue with those who doubt the whole from without or major parts of it from within. Since many do not know of, hold to, or care about dogmatic matters as they bear on social and economic life, we have to show the significance of theology in and for public discourse.

We do this in a dialogical setting and for the dialogical settings of teaching and learning. Supported by the Project on Public Theology at Princeton Theological Seminary and the Lilly Endowment, our editorial board gathers twice a year for discussion, and each volume will have three or more perspectives on its topic. The Board and all contributors are Christian, and all have studied the relationship of Christian ethics to economic life. We come from several backgrounds and traditions—Ecumenical, Evangelical, and Roman Catholic. Most are Protestant. We represent several fields of study. Not every position is present. No one is flatly a libertarian, humanist, liberationist, or fundamentalist, although members of our group are convinced that, with proper theological qualification, one or another of these views can make a contribution to some aspect of our thought together. Taken alone, these views tend to be reductionistic, dishonest, and unfaithful. Yet, we also suspect that each of these views poses a question that must be answered: What preserves individual dignity? What place do we give to humanist values and to the place of humanity in the plenitude of creation? What serves the poor and the oppressed? And, what is fundamental in faith and morals?

We are believers seeking to identify the ethics for economic reconstruction. Less like talk-shows or party platforms where people vent opinions to gain power than like seminars or discussion groups where people study important matters from different angles, we try to plumb deeper, seek a truer view, and find a better way for the common life. We invite all who will to join us.

Max L. Stackhouse
General Editor

Already Published

Christian Social Ethics in a Global Era
Max L. Stackhouse, with Peter L. Berger,
Dennis P. McCann, and M. Douglas Meeks

In Preparation

The Business Corporation and Productive Justice
David A. Krueger, with Donald W. Shriver, Jr., and Laura L. Nash

Organization Man, Organization Woman:
Calling, Leadership, and Culture
Shirley J. Roels, with Paul Camenisch and Barbara Andolsen

Other Volumes to Be Announced

Introduction

Max L. Stackhouse

Among the matters that today bind the world together in a new way is a fresh awareness of the ecological issue. In spite of the divisions people experience regarding communities and regions, class and sex, cultures and societies, ethnic groups and nations, we live in a common bio-physical universe. Recognize, honor, or celebrate all the diversities we find within and among us and the distinctiveness which we find in the plethora of things around us as we will, it remains true that we are all a part of a vast interdependent web of existence. That may not be all we are, but the bio-physical is woven into what we are.

Ecological awareness is not the only issue that binds us together today. All over the world, the natural and social sciences are used to define the way the world is and to make it better (even if some postmodernists claim that the sciences themselves are more social constructions than descriptions). Further, constitutional democracy with provisions for human rights is more widespread than ever before in history (which some rightly see as subversive of traditional authority), while media, communications, and the world internet link more people in more locales with more other people in other locales than ever before (eroding the sovereignty of each self-centered society). Each of these cuts more deeply into the world as it must have been prior to human intervention.

These changes make the world more open to doing business; and a global economy led by the transnational corporations draws ever greater portions of the population into a global market that involves both new ties and new competition for resources, jobs, capital, and customers—and thus economic dislocation for some. Indeed, a new set of political economic institutions generated in the last half century—

e.g., the World Bank, the International Monetary Fund, and the more recent World Trade Organization—signal a fresh consensus about how production and distribution can most effectively aid human development (although these institutions are resisted in some areas of the world).

But it is not at all clear what all these other commonalities mean in regard to the "carrying capacity" of the earth's resources; and many who have opposed contemporary economic developments on traditionalist, socialist, or naturalist grounds have turned to the environmental movements as one of the last arenas to resist and oppose what they view as the exploitation of the world by the forces of capitalism. This is true in spite of the fact that it becomes increasingly easy to make the case that traditional, socialist, and naturalistic societies have played great havoc with the environment and that those countries where corporations have flourished seem to have both the economic resources and the legal structures of accountability to help clean up messes, as was suggested in the first volume of this series.

Still, the issues of ecology frequently are taken to have a priority over other social concerns by many. After all, it is asked, what could be more wholistic, more comprehending? What could be more fateful for our survival? What could more clearly call us to rid personal and social practices of egocentric tendencies and to assume moral responsibility for the well-being of the world and future generations?

It is not, however, only a contest between what is "natural" in the discovered world and the natural tendency of humans to rearrange their environment. Over the ages, most of humanity has held that the very nature of both humanity and the bio-physical universe invites not only moral responsibility by means of a natural law, but acknowledgement of a spiritual mystery deeper than the facts of nature itself. Are all the world's great religions mistaken when they claim that the vast plenitude of being has a profound spiritual force behind it, and that its superficially apparent chaos is comprehended by a real, if extremely complex, order and sustained by a discernible, if incredibly subtle, blend of purposes? It was, many say, created by God, and traces of divine order and purpose can be found in it.

Such convictions raise the ante as to how we treat our material environment. Everything turns out to be at stake in the issues; not only the earth itself, but humanity and the very will of God. And if it should become clear that our sciences, our constitutions, our view of rights, our business transactions, our technologies, our international regulative institutions, or our religions should prove to lead us to ecological disaster, would we not have to change them?

But if we agree that this is so, do we not admit that "nature" does not rule the way things are, that we have to take charge of them? Calling upon humanity to take responsibility for the bio-physical world presumes an extraordinary technological-managerial competence and a nearly complete human capability to alter the course of nature. And if that is true, whence do we derive the models of how we think things ought to be? They cannot come from either nature or history, for these are what we seek to change.

In fact, most of the ways by which we deal with ecological issues do not involve abandoning or changing the total fabric of human civilization with its technological engagements and basic religious convictions so much as extending them in ways that enhance the environment as a human habitat in the long run, as we bring more of the world under human cultivation and simultaneously try to live in accord with the order and purpose God intended. But that implies a willingness to intervene in, modify, and sometimes reshape the bio-physical order for the sake of humankind. And, for all the commonalities that bind the world together today, the questions of whether and, if so, how much we should do so, and on what terms we might do so, are hotly debated.

How shall we sort the decisive questions? Many of them can be identified, but how to weigh the factors once they are sorted remains a problem. For example, it is not difficult to recognize that, looked at macroscopically, very decisive issues are at stake regarding the relative importance of the bio-physical realm, the realm of human societies, cultures, and civilizations, and the realm of God and God's will for creation and humanity.

Ancient myths spoke of a three-tiered universe: the lowest level was the earth, under and around us; the middle level was that of human life in community; and the highest level was the overarching domain of the divine. We are, as was said long ago, "more than the beasts but less than the angels." In a full cosmology, of course, these levels all interact, and a decisive question for centuries has been how we are to understand the relative power, influence, and authority of these three levels for human existence.

It turns out that those ancient insights are not far removed from certain decisive questions present in the ecological issues today. This volume begins, like all the books in this series, with a lead essay that attempts to define the critical questions in one or another area of ethics and economic life, and is followed by responses that provide critical or alternative perspectives. The lead essay in this volume, by Thomas Derr, takes humanity as the center point of analysis. It is, to be sure, a distinctive understanding of humanity as can be seen in the term "Christian Humanism" in his title, but that is because he believes that Christianity offers the best interpretation of what it means to be human. It is a humanity that is understood both in relationship to God, but also in an ethical relationship to the ecological order.

On the basis of this perspective, Derr holds that a wide range of ecologists distort the picture of humanity by submerging human life into "nature," ignoring human transcendence over it. To make his case, he not only looks at what many ecologists say when they speak of these matters, but at the kinds of spectacles that they wear to view the world the way they do. He is convinced that these spectacles are badly ground, and thus parts of their vision are distorted.

In a sharply stated response, James Nash claims that it is Derr who does not see the issues clearly, because he is much too focused on a confidence in human nature and, indeed, on the capacity of modern, technological civilizations to meet key challenges of the new ecological awareness. Clearly, Nash doubts that Derr has found the correct balance of earth, humanity, and divinity.

Richard Neuhaus agrees with Derr that the balance between the "naturalistic" and the "humanistic" interpretations of our world have been much too lopsided on the naturalistic side by recent ecological advocates. But he is not sure that Derr (or the more radical ecological advocates) has a complete or accurate picture of the place of divinity in all this. In fact, he presses Derr to develop a Christology in which the normative relation of the human and divine is made more articulate. That, he suggests, would strengthen Derr's hands against those who would divinize nature, but it would also call his humanism, even his explicitly theological variety, to become more precise about the place of God in the whole picture.

At least two other issues are embedded in, and cross-cut, these debates. One is the question of the relationship of "creation" to "nature." It is fascinating to see how much the deep traditions that inform these thinkers show up in their very contemporary arguments. Both Nash, as a "liberal" United Methodist, and Neuhaus, as

14

a "conservative" Roman Catholic, represent traditions that have had, in distinctive ways, rather more optimistic views of "nature" than does Derr, as a "moderate" Reformed thinker. The tradition Nash represents frequently takes the modern, sometimes Romantic, view of nature very seriously, and that of Neuhaus usually holds that ancient views of natural law are indispensable to a complete theology and ethic. Derr, it seems, is more rooted in the classical Reformed "creational" tradition, which is more pessimistic about "nature" than both of these. While all things bear the traces of an original goodness, as God intended, much of nature is fallen, in need of stewardly constraint and reconstruction. Thus, the ethical estimate of the place of technology in human civilization, and its potential for human interventions in nature is higher in many parts of the Reformed tradition than in both the more naturalistic, liberal forms of Protestantism, and the sacramental traditions of the Catholic heritage. In the Reformed view, we have a more emphatic duty under God to use the gift of intelligence to intervene in the brokenness of nature, to manage it, and to bring "fallen nature" more closely to the order and purposes of the Creator. Derr's modesty in stating his case does not hide his Reformed commitments.

At still another level, one can speak of the tensions within the entire ecological debate as to who or what is to decide the ways in which we should weight these matters. All three of these authors are deeply involved in "intermediary institutions." All are more than private citizens in that they speak often in the public arena and about public issues. Yet, none is employed by government or corporations that deal directly with ecological questions. The reader can see that each of these authors places his confidence on different parts of the common life as the best locus for dealing with the issues.

On the whole, Nash wants the churches to put pressure on government to assume leadership in this area, while Neuhaus sees a much larger role for the church and its doctrine, and a lesser role for government. Compared with these two arguments, Derr places greater emphasis on the institutions of civil society. The church and politics have, of course, roles to play; but the university and the corporation, the media, and the citizenry are central to the formation of a moral consensus that, on this issue, will influence both church and government.

In any case, such matters make many of the current debates about "individualism" vs. "communitarianism" less significant than the question about which kinds of social institutions are decisive agents in dealing with such matters. In brief, behind each of the views represented here is not only a general theory of the bio-physical world in relationship to humanity and to God, but also an implied theory of how society ought to be organized to be most responsible for the earth, under God.

In a rejoinder, Derr responds to the charges by Nash and the suggestions by Neuhaus, and it becomes clear that very profound differences exist about how we are, under God, to view the nature of nature and the nature of human nature as we look to the future. The intensity of disagreement sometimes erupts into very sharp comments in the present volume, nearly disrupting the possibilities of an ongoing civil discussion. But the discussion and debate does continue here, and bears within it most of the unresolved issues on these questions that continue to haunt church and society, community and public policy, individual convictions and international debates. It is a wonderful testimony to the quality of the contributions that we have before us.

Chapter 1

Environmental Ethics and Christian Humanism

Thomas Sieger Derr

What Sort of Argument Is This?

Environmental philosophers are extremely fond of typologies; or perhaps, given their biological bent, we should say "phyla" or species divisions. They love classifications such as "eco-holism" or "eco-compatibilism" or even "eco-humanism," not to say more standard pigeonholes like "radical" and "moderate."

Reading one such list not too long ago I came across the category to which, in their eyes, this book should no doubt be assigned: "unreconstructed anthropocentrism." The appellation was not meant kindly. The direction of environmental philosophy for years now has been hostile to the human race, regarding our preference for our own kind as the true source of environmental degradation. Even Christian environmentalists have joined the choir, arguing for rights of nature against humans, denying human priority in God's sight, succumbing, as I will argue below, to a fatalism which regards the end of the human species as a likely expression of the divine will.

There have been so many books and essays in this mode that another work along these lines would risk redundancy. This one doesn't. It rather stubbornly and against the stream reiterates the anthropocentric viewpoint that I defended twenty-five years ago in *Ecology and Human Need*, in a time when books on environmental ethics were few and far between. This essay is thus not only "unreconstructed," but unrepentant. From the point of view of mainstream environmentalism that may mean that, as a practical matter, when comes the Green Revolution, I will be sent to the countryside to work off my sins in a reeducation camp.

So be it. Actually I do not mind being called an anthropocentrist, though I would rather say simply "humanist," meaning that my priority in matters ecological is humankind. But then, so as not to be confused with the excitable and strident folks who publish anti-religious manifestos, I insist on the all-important adjective: I am a *Christian* humanist. What follows is written from an expressly Christian viewpoint, steeped in a deep and lifelong commitment to the church.

Besides admitting to my worldview, I should also confess to two methodological prejudices. One is modesty. This essay has a very modest approach, despite the efforts of the anti-human "biocen-trists" to paint us humanists as wicked and arrogant. I start with human concerns because I do not know the cosmic intent or whether there is value in the natural world without the human race (except, as I will say, that I trust God values his creation). I cannot "think like a mountain" (Aldo Leopold), much less like God, and had better not claim that I can. I learned early in life, from my brilliant but modest father, to say "I don't know" when I really don't. I begin modestly with what I do know, that we humans are valuing creatures and that we value our own existence. So I use "anthropocentrism," that dread word, not from pride or arrogance, but precisely for the sake of modesty.

My other prejudice is simplicity. I have a fondness for "Occam's razor"; in general, if an explanation is simple, it is better. I acknowledge that physicists are more fond of this principle than biologists, and that the truth sometimes does lie in complexity. Still, it seems better to me not to introduce complications where they are not needed.

Adherence to these two principles will, I hope, keep this work from overstatement. And so to my argument.

The Challenge of Biocentrism

At first glance I must appear to be an unlikely person to be critical of the environmental movement in any way. A sometime country-man, I usually know where the wind is, and what phase of the moon we are in. I take good care of my small woodland, and I love my dogs. My personal predilections carry over into public policy, too. I champion the goals of reducing the waste stream, improving air and water quality, preserving the forests, protecting wildlife. I think of environmentalism in some form as a necessary and inevitable movement.

But by current standards that does not make me much of an environmentalist, for I am profoundly unhappy with the direction of current environmental philosophy, and most especially because I am a Christian. My trouble stems partly from the determination of mainstream environmentalism to blame Christianity for whatever ecological trouble we are in. That contributes enough to my discomfort that I am going to take a moment right now to dismiss it before getting on to matters of principle. It is a piece of historical nonsense which apparently thrives on repetition, so that every time it appears in print more people feel free to quote the source as authoritative, and each reference has a multiplier effect.

I

Although something like this cannot surely be traced to a single source, probably the closest we can come to the origin of this canard is an essay by the late, formidable medieval historian Lynn White, Jr., "The Historical Roots of Our Ecologic Crisis," which appeared originally in 1967,[1] and has since enjoyed virtually eternal life in anthologies. It is not so much that White himself blamed Christianity; he was far too careful a historian for that, and moreover, he wrote as a Christian and an active churchman himself. But his essay was used by others with darker purposes, others who seized upon his suggestive lines and ran away with them.

To be sure, White gave them ammunition. He traced the modern technological exploitation of nature back through the ages to the famous "dominion" passage in Genesis 1:28, which gives humanity some form of supremacy over the rest of creation. Because, he argued, technology is now ecologically "out of control," it is fair to say that "Christianity bears a huge burden of guilt" for this result. We need to reject "the Christian axiom that nature has no reason for existence save to serve man." We must overcome our "orthodox Christian arrogance toward nature." He even gave his blessing to the counter-culture's affinity for alternative religions: "More science and more technology are not going to get us out of the present ecologic crisis until we find a new religion, or rethink our old one . . . The hippies . . . show a sound instinct in their affinity for Zen Buddhism and Hinduism, which conceive the man-nature relationship as very nearly the mirror image of the Christian view." Small wonder that this essay has been cited by others who are not fond of the Church, who can say with assurance, as does George Sessions, premier philosopher of the currently popular "deep ecology" movement, "The environmental crisis [is] fundamentally a crisis of the West's anthropocentric philosophical and religious orientations and values."[2]

Is Christianity really the ecological culprit? And did White really say that it is? The answer is no to both questions.

Many scholars have concluded that Christianity made an important contribution to the rise of science and technology in the West, but it would be too much to make it the only cause. Yes, the doctrine of creation separates nature from God, makes creation not itself divine, and suggests strongly that inquiry into its workings is a pious study of the mind of the Maker. That way of looking at the world surely abets the scientific and technological culture, but is not a *sufficient* condition for its appearance; that culture did not arise in lands dominated by Eastern Christianity, but only in the Latin West, and then only after a millennium. Nor is it a *necessary* condition, for science flourished without benefit of Christianity in China, ancient Greece, and medieval Islam.

Neither can we say that it is chiefly Christian lands which are environmentally heedless. Ecological destruction like overgrazing and deforestation, sometimes enough to cause the fall of civilizations, has been committed by Egyptians, Persians, Romans, Aztecs, Indians, even Buddhists, to no one's surprise, probably, except those gullible Westerners who romanticize other cultures of which they know very little. There is, for example, the noted Western ecologist Paul Ehrlich who, despising his own civilization, extols "the Eastern and gentle Pacific cultures in which man lives (or lived) a leisurely life of harmony with nature."[3] That could only have been written by someone who knows little of the sorry, violent history of those peoples.

What, then, does produce the technological society? And what causes ecological pillage? As to technology, we may guess at primitive origins in simple artisanship and the domestication of animals; the natural human quest for labor-saving devices; trade and commerce with other societies where these developments are further advanced; or just the natural momentum of technological change once started in however small a way, i.e. one thing leading naturally to another. Other likely suspects include geography, climate, population growth, urbanism, and democracy. To this mix add the idea that the world is an intelligible order ruled by general principles that we have received from the ancient Greeks, mediated powerfully (as A. N. Whitehead asserted) by the medieval insistence on the rationality of God; or perhaps the rise of purely *secular* philosophy celebrating human mastery over nature, as in Bacon, Descartes, and Leibnitz. That is quite a list. It would be impossible, given this wealth of candidates, to sort out what the primary influences really are, and even White acknowledged that the causes are finally mysterious.

As for the causes of ecological harm, we may cite first the simple fact that there now are more people on the earth than ever before, whose common search for food and shelter frequently assaults the world around them. It is, notably, not only the factories of the developed nations, but the daily gathering and burning of wood for fuel by rural people in the poorer countries, along with the depredations of their domestic animals, which has damaged the world's soils and makes their air far more polluted than ours. Of course industrial development has caused ecological damage, but much of that is the result of ignorance and error, mistakes often quite correctable. There are noisy voices in the environmental movement who attribute the damage to corporate greed without remainder, and the more fanciful among them go searching for deeper roots in capitalist culture, which in turn they find spawned by Christian theology in some form. But it is simpler and surely more accurate to say that human self-seeking is a constant in our natures, and that no culture, no matter what its religion, has managed successfully to eliminate it.

White really did not blame Christianity for our environmental difficulties. By "orthodox Christian attitude toward nature," he did *not* mean, he said, that arrogance toward nature is orthodox Christian doctrine, only that presumably orthodox Christians have been arrogant toward nature. By "the Christian axiom that nature has no reason for existence save to serve man," he meant, he claimed, that some Christians have *regarded* it as an axiom, not that it is a matter of true faith.[4] Qualifications like these really vitiate the apparent argument in "Historical Roots," which was that Christians were heedless of nature *because* they were Christians. But on reflection, after absorbing the storm, White retreated to saying only that Christians, like human beings everywhere, found it possible to misappropriate certain elements from their religious tradition to serve their selfish ends.

I had the opportunity to talk with White at some length about

21

his essay and have reason to believe that although he may have been pleased at the notice his piece received, he was also disturbed at the way it was used. He was only half-joking when he wrote me about the "theology of ecology," saying, "Of course, I claim to be the founder!" But surely he would disown many of his offspring, and that brings me to those matters of principle I mentioned earlier.

II

What is the real, orthodox Christian attitude toward nature? It is, in a word, stewardship. We are trustees for that which does not belong to us. "The earth is the Lord's, and the fullness thereof, the world and they that dwell therein." "All that is in the heavens and in the earth is thine." The implications of this idea for environmentalism are profound and, I think, wholly positive, and have been spelled out in different ways by many writers, including Douglas John Hall in *The Steward*, Loren Wilkinson and his colleagues in *Earthkeeping in the Nineties*, and my own *Ecology and Human Need*.[5] Wilkinson's succinct definition is this: "Stewardship [is] the exercise of delegated dominion in the service of creation."[6]

We should not shy away from the word "dominion," though it has often, perhaps usually, been read by hostile environmentalists as if it were "domination."[7] Made "in the image of God," humans are definitely above nature and in charge, but our primacy is one of responsibility. We cannot do whatever pleases us. Our dominion is exercised for the benefit of the true owner, as God's stewards. It is an act of *service* to the creation, as both Wilkinson and Hall point out.[8]

Of course we cannot serve and honor the creation by destroying it. But neither are we meant to preserve it exactly as we found it, freezing it in original perfection, so to speak, although this is sometimes treated as an environmental goal.[9] Genesis 2:15 says that Adam was placed in the garden "to till it and keep it": it has to be worked to be properly "kept," and if it is to feed him. Gardeners do not leave things as they found them. (Pastor, admiring parishioner's garden: "John, you and the Lord have done wonderful things with this garden." John: "Yes, but you should have seen the mess when the Lord had it all alone.") The steward's task is responsible development. Remember that Jesus scolds as "wicked and slothful" the servant who buries the talent entrusted to him, without developing and growing it.

Stewardship of the earth, then, means that we have an obligation to care for it as a fit habitat for human beings, to preserve the systems on which our life depends, to treat the non-human creation with respect and to use it properly for human need, and to develop it and manage change without doing violence to the fundamental structure of life. Our commitment and our duty is to love the world both for our own sakes, and for love of its Maker. "Every one to whom much is given, of him will much be required," said Jesus, describing the role of the steward; "and of him to whom men commit much they will demand the more."[10]

The rough historical evidence suggests that this theoretical obligation has not been without its practical results. There have, for example, been Christian lands in Europe farmed in an ecologically stable manner for centuries. René Dubos says flatly, "The Judeo-Christian peoples were probably the first to develop on a large scale a pervasive concern for land management and an ethic of nature."[11] Clarence Glacken, one of the most patient and exhaustive historians of these matters, concludes from his survey of the vast literature, "I am convinced that modern ecological theory . . . owes its origin to the design argument," the idea so prominent in Christian theology of all ages that the complexity of the world is the work of a creator God.[12] Lynn White knew this, too. And in the past it has been common for even the ecological critics of Christianity to say that the Christians' problem is only that they did not take their own doctrines seriously enough.

What is new in our world today is a rejection of this semi-or pseudo-irenic view and its replacement with a root-and-branch attack on the doctrine of stewardship itself by that increasingly powerful and pervasive school of environmental thought known as biocentrism. Of course it has many variations, and one must be careful not to over-generalize. But it is fair to say of nearly all varieties that they find the idea of stewardship repulsively anthropocentric, implying as it plainly does that humans are in charge of nature, meant to manage it for purposes which humans alone are able to perceive. Stewardship, says Richard Sylvan (ex-Routley), means "Man as tyrant."[13] Should we, following the command to Adam, think of ourselves as the earth's gardeners? Bad metaphor: gardening is controlling the earth's fecundity in a way that nature, left to its own devices, would not behave. Human design is wrongly imposed.

The problem is simply compounded by Christian theism, which

places humans at the apex of nature by design of the ultimate giver of life. When we say we are made in the image of God, we give ourselves license to claim that our interests as a species take precedence over the rest of creation, the stewardship of which means mainly that we should manage it so that it sustains us indefinitely. Nature is made for us, as we are made for God. Here, say the biocentrists, is the bitter harvest of anthropocentrism: human selfishness, parochialism, chauvinism, "speciesism" (the awful term, apparently originally coined by Richard Ryder, which Peter Singer uses of those who reject animal rights), moral naiveté, a profanation of nature, self-importance, and pride carried to their extreme. Regarding humans as having more inherent worth than other species is, says Paul Taylor, like regarding noblemen as having more inherent worth than peasants. A claim to human superiority is "a deep-seated prejudice . . . a wholly arbitrary claim . . . an irrational bias in our own favor."[14] Lynn White was right after all: it is simply arrogance.

What do the biocentrists propose instead? Their most fundamental proposition is that nature itself, the life process as a whole, is the primary locus of value. Within that process all species have value, intrinsic value, just because they *are*, because they would not *be* if they did not have an appropriate niche in the ecology of the whole. And if they have intrinsic value, we must say that they have rights of some sort, claims on us for appropriate treatment, an integrity of their own that is not available for our mere willful disposition.

Notice that the alleged rights of nonhuman entities do not depend on their possession of any specific attributes, like rationality, or language, or even sentience. That would be subtle anthropocentrism, say the biocentrists. It would make a semblance to human characteristics the test of value—a mistake many of the animal rights advocates make and which, as we will see in the next section, separates them from the biocentrists. We must say instead that all entities have value simply in themselves. They have their own purposes, or "good," which they value, either consciously or unconsciously. Their value, and their consequent rights, depends solely on their essential needs to be themselves, on their own "vital interests."

Since the assertion that the natural world has rights which we must honor begins with the claim that it has intrinsic value, let us spend a moment on this prior claim. No one, to my knowledge, has worked harder, or with more care, or with more gracefully expressed formulations, to establish the idea that natural entities have value

24

independent of humans (or for that matter, independent of God, whom he does not mention in his major work) than Holmes Rolston. To Rolston the ability to support life is a natural good which the earth possesses without us, which means that the human experience of satisfaction is not necessary to have a "good." The earth is able to produce value without us. We recognize the presence of that objective value when we value our natural science, "for no study of a worthless thing can be intrinsically valuable."[15] Organisms are living beings and hence have a good for themselves, maintaining their own life; and this good is a value that can claim our respect. In fact, "the living individual . . . is per se an intrinsic value."[16]

Rolston admits that the human participant supplies value to an object: "No value can in principle . . . be altogether independent of a valuing consciousness . . . If all consciousness were annihilated at a stroke, there would be no good or evil, . . . no right or wrong; only impassive phenomena would remain." However, "to say that something is valuable means that it is able to be valued if and when human valuers come along, but it has this property whether or not humans . . . ever arrive." The value is already in the thing, hence "intrinsic." He does not like any account of value in natural things that depends on human psychology. He wants the value to emerge from nature directly, so that we can value the object "for what it is in itself." Value may increase with the attention of humans, but it is present without them. Thus his theory is "biocentric."[17]

Other fine, though theologically innocent, expressions of this viewpoint include Lawrence Johnson's *A Morally Deep World*, which bases a theory of value on interests. If a thing has interests it has "moral significance." Any living thing, Johnson argues, including plants, species, and whole ecosystems (he *can* see the forest for the trees), but not rocks or machines, has interests, at the very least in surviving. An interest is what a thing requires for its own "well-being" quite independent of its ability to express its concern in language or conceptualize it in thought. Johnson's key assumption is that these interests must command our ethical respect to some degree, even when they are proper to non-human entities.[18]

There are many variations on these themes, of course, whose subtleties fill the pages of learned journals. But let us cut the exposition short at this point and answer the general argument. Against the attribution of intrinsic value to natural objects, I argue that, on the contrary, with the important theistic exception noted below, we hu-

25

mans supply the value, that nature is valuable because we find it so. There is no value without a valuer. Values are for someone or some thing. A thing can provide value to someone, and in that sense it has or possesses value, i.e. the capacity to provide value for someone. That is not the same as "intrinsic" value, which is value in and for the thing itself, whatever anyone makes of it. Simply because we value studying something does not make it intrinsically valuable; it makes it valuable *for us*. Someone may find it extremely valuable for his peace of mind to finger worry beads, but that does not mean that we must accord those beads intrinsic value. Some elderly recluses have been known to save newspapers for years, valuing the accumulating mountain highly. But that does not make these old papers *intrinsically* valuable.

Of course these are inanimate matter. What about living entities? An organism may have a goal or drive for itself in perpetuating its life, an "interest" in survival, like mosquitoes or bacteria; but that is quite different from having an intrinsic value which other, conscious beings are required to acknowledge. I see no reason why I should pay moral attention to a microorganism that intends me harm. Subtract the ascription of moral significance to these life forms, however, consider ethics as a human affair, and the confusion is eliminated.

The attempt of Rolston and other biocentrists—J. Baird Callicott, for example—to distinguish between human appreciation of nature's intrinsic value, and the value which humans add to it by appreciating it, is splitting too fine a hair for my taste. It is much more compelling and credible to say simply that a natural object may generate value for us not by itself but only in conjunction with our situation. We supply the value; the object contributes its being. Value is not a term appropriate to it in isolation, by itself.

The discussion of value takes a different course if we are theists who accept the doctrine of creation as the foundation of our environmental philosophy, or theology. We say, as James Nash rightly does, that all creatures must reflect their Maker in some way, and that a presumption of value in their favor is not unreasonable.[19] This is not to say that natural entities have intrinsic value; their value still depends on the valuer. But here the valuer is other than human beings. God bestows the value, which still does not belong to the object as such.

This is a well-developed idea with impeccable Thomist credentials, yet it does not solve our ecological problem. If anything, it makes it more difficult. To say that "God saw everything that he had made, and behold, it was very good," establishes well our obligation to respect the natural world; it is, of course, the foundation of our stewardship duty. But we still face the observable amorality of nature and its frequent hostility to us, and in a peculiarly painful form, for it raises the ancient problem of theodicy. That nature is full of what we perceive as violence and ugliness is beyond dispute. It is the realm of the food chain, of brute struggle and painful death. Surprisingly, no one has put it more candidly and vividly than Rolston himself:

> Wildness is a gigantic food pyramid, and this sets value in a grim, deathbound jungle. Earth is a slaughterhouse, with life a miasma rising over the stench. Nothing is done for the benefit of another. . . . Blind and ever urgent exploitation is nature's driving theme.[20]

Worse yet, from our point of view, nature is frequently hostile to our human lives. From violent storm to volcanic eruption to drought to killer viruses, to say nothing of the cosmic possibilities that could end our lives in one great, sudden bang, the natural world is certainly not unambiguously our friend.

Can one read an ethic out of this natural behavior? Not likely, or at least not an ethic which any Christian could for a moment tolerate. It is not that nature is immoral, for to say that would be to read our human values into this world. But nature is certainly amoral, and we could not begin to derive our ethical standards from its actions. Nevertheless the biocentrists, bound to locate value primarily in this amoral world, find something to cherish there, something which rises above the brutality of the food chain, something which relativizes the ugliness. Some choose harmony, which they profess to see behind the apparent chaos, patterns which repeat themselves, balances that are restored. Others admire nature's vitality, fecundity, and regenerative power, or its strength, endurance, and dynamism, even in the midst of its fury. New life emerges from rotting carcasses and burned forests. "Ugliness," says Rolston, "though present at time in particulars, is not the last word. . . . Over time nature will bring beauty out of this ugliness."[21]

But seeing matters thus is a matter of choice. Harmony in an ecosystem is only apparent, superficial. There are emergent forces that triumph, species that disappear, balances that are permanently upset. Nature destroys that which does not fit its designs for survival. To see harmony is to look selectively. Harmony, like beauty, is mostly in the eye of the beholder. If it is natural power and regenerative strength that enthrall us, we can love the rapid reproduction of cancer cells, or the terrible beauty of a tornado. We can love what kills us. Over time, nature means to destroy this world. The death of our sun star might be beautiful if there were anyone to see it, I suppose, even though it will mark the end of planet earth. We can appreciate the natural facts any way we choose. To say it once again, we supply the value.

But what shall we say to those theists who reply that surely God must value what he has made? Can we discern what God intends for the creation? Rolston, wearing his theological hat and speaking to Christians, suggests that we may apply to nature as well as to humans the major themes of the Christian story, that new life arises from old, that good comes from evil, that suffering has a transformative character.[22] This is a daring idea, but, I think, wrong. The Christian themes in fact deal with human beings, and it is an impermissible leap, a kind of theological anthropomorphism, to apply them to non-human nature, attractive though the idea is at first glance. The concept of redemptive suffering can only apply to nature by analogy, and I doubt any literal reading of the comparison can be legitimate.

Faced with the puzzle of natural evil and the ancient lineage of the problem of theodicy, and bearing in mind the centuries of false prophets who have claimed to know God's will all too well, I think we must be very, very modest in talking about God's intention for nature. Given the centrality of the divine-human drama in Christian faith, given its proclamation of the redemptive event addressed to humankind, I am certainly willing to say—more than willing, in fact, insistent upon saying—that our focus must be on human life, and that our task with the earth is to sustain the conditions for human life as far into the future as our wits and strength allow. But I am not willing to go much beyond that. I am not willing to guess at what the earth's good is, or, put better, to guess at what God intends for the earth, which by definition would be its good.

The biocentrists are much less modest. They do claim to know the good of nature. If I may turn the tables on them, I would say they are far more daring, even impudent, in their claims to know the purposes of nature (or of God with nature, if they are theists) than are traditional Christians. Building on their theory of intrinsic value in natural entities, the biocentrists tell us that there are severe limits on what we may do with the natural world. In search of a strong position that will have sufficient force to restrain human selfishness, many of them, though not all, adopt the language of rights. Nature has rights, and thus claims against us, much as we humans claim rights which other humans may not transgress.

But at once they plunge us into a realm of competing rights. Whose rights take precedence? When may they be violated, and by whom? May we eat meat? experiment on animals in laboratories? spread agricultural pesticides? use antibiotics? dam rivers? May a cat kill a mouse? In order to solve these conflicts, and save the whole concept from reduction to absurdity, its defenders propose an inequality of rights, or even a complete disjunction between our obligations to each other and to the natural world.

Constructing a calculus of variable rights for different levels of existence is no simple task, however. Nash, who calls himself a Christian biocentrist and who, for his theological care, deserves to be exempted from many of the faults of the larger movement, does it by using "value-creating" and "value-experiencing" as the criteria for relevant differences, with rights diminishing as we descend a scale established by the relative presence of these capacities. Thus he hopes to solve conflicts of rights by "appropriate adjustments for the different contexts."[23] Similarly, Rolston would have the rights of animals and other natural entities "fade over a descending phylogenic spectrum."[24]

Johnson, acknowledging that some interests have more weight than others, gives preference to those of more developed creatures, thus clearly favoring human beings. All interests count, he insists, but his expression of the point is carefully qualified: "While different beings have different interests, there is no viable and non-arbitrary reason why—when everything else is equal—the interests of one being ought to take precedence over the *equivalent* interests of another being."[25] His maxim is "Give due respect to the interests of all beings that have interests, in proportion to their interests."[26] When this principle is applied, however, lesser creatures don't stand much of a chance against their superiors, although their odds increase considerably if their whole species is threatened. A plant's interest in not being eaten is "much slighter" than our interest in eating it; and, not surprisingly, our interest in avoiding smallpox is much greater than that organism's (very real) interest in surviving:

> Individuals toward the lower end of the scale have much less of a well-being to be enhanced or infringed. . . . Individuals higher up the scale merit more individual consideration. Sentience, preferences, and rationality would give us indications of greater moral significance.[27]

In constructing the scale, in determining the measures, we inevitably stumble across familiar, anthropocentric qualities like reason and language. These systems, then, all give priority in rights to humans, a lower priority to creatures merely sentient, and still less to nonsentient entities. More radical versions take a Schweitzer-like approach, avoiding all killing of "lesser" forms of life except under threat to our own lives, and then only with a profound sense of sorrow for this necessary evil. How many times have we heard it said in recent years, with wondering admiration, that American Indians, those supposed ecological paragons, apologized to their game before killing it? An Irish pacifist once told me, with appropriate sardonic tone, that political assassination in Ireland was so common it was considered a normal part of the political process, not murder in the sense of violating the sixth commandment; "but," he added, "it is doubtful whether the victims appreciated the distinction." And so also the caribou, slain by an Indian arrow tipped with a profound apology.

Faced with these tangles, it must be tempting even for the biocentrically-inclined to give up on rights language. Rolston verges on the cynical when he admits that rights may after all be merely "a cultural discovery, really a convention," that does not translate to ecosystems, but that it may be politically useful to use the term anyway. "It is sometimes convenient rhetorically but in principle unnecessary to use the concept of rights at all."[28] What matters is the power of the restraint, and the language may be adjusted as necessary.

With all due respect to the intellectual strength and agility of the biocentric arguments, I would slice through their Gordian tangles by limiting "rights" to intra-human affairs. "Rights" is a political and social term in the first instance, applicable only to human society, often enshrined in a fundamental document like a constitution, or embedded in the common law. As a metaphysical term, the transcultural phrase "human rights" applies to that which belongs to human beings by their very nature, i.e. not by their citizenship. Theologically, we guarantee human rights neither by our nature nor our citizenship, but by the radical equality of the love of God, the concept of "alien dignity," a grace bestowed on us which does not belong to our humanness as such. In none of these forms has nature participated in rights.

Biocentrists sometimes seek to redress what to them are these deficiencies in the history of ideas by what I will call the argument from extension. "Rights," they point out, originally applied only to male citizens; but just as rights were gradually extended to women, to slaves, and finally to all other human beings, so it is a logical extension of this political liberalism to extend rights now to nonhuman creatures and even to agglomerations like ecosystems. Or, if the forum is not politics but Christian ethics, one could argue that commands to love our neighbors must now apply to nonhuman "neighbors," our "co-siblings of creation,"[29] or that the justice we are obliged to dispense to the poor and oppressed must also now be extended to oppressed nature, or even that the enemies we are asked to love may include nature in its most hostile modes.

Although I understand and appreciate the generous spirit of this line of argument, I think it involves a serious category mistake. Nonhumans cannot have the moral status that only humans possess by our very natures. It is not irrelevant that the command to love our neighbors, in its original context, does in fact *not* apply to nonhumans. An "extension" amounts to a substantial misreading of the text. Our obligations to the natural world cannot be expressed this way.

Another use of the idea of extension, which occurs in Nash and in a different way in Paul Santmire,[30] is to argue that ultimate redemption is meant not only for humans, but also for the natural world, indeed the whole cosmos. That in turn would imply much about our treatment of nature, our companion in cosmic redemption. The Incarnation confers dignity not only on us, but on the whole material world; the divine takes on not only human flesh, but material being in general. There are certain New Testament passages which are suggestive here (Rom. 8:18-25, Col. 1:15-20, Rev. 21:1), and Eastern Orthodox theology has formally incorporated this notion as a virtual "deification" of matter.

This is a theological idea of considerable gravity, and it deserves to be taken seriously. Nevertheless the doctrine is only vaguely expressed and appears to faith as hope, a hope made legitimate by faith, but a hope without details. Indeed, if we are to be scientifically honest, it is a "hope against hope," given the secular geological wisdom about the death of planet earth in fire and ice. The doctrine of eschatological renewal, while it certainly underscores the honor and respect we owe to God's creation, cannot tell us much about the care of nature beyond what we already know from our stewardship obligation, that we are to preserve this world as habitat fit for humanity. The natural details of a redeemed environment are beyond our ken. Our trust in God for the eternal Presence beyond death does not require the preservation of these rocks and rills, these woods and templed hills. Again we find ourselves behind the veil of ignorance: we simply do not know nature's divine destiny.

In short, and in sum thus far, I believe it would be more consistent, more logical, and conceptually much simpler to insist that nature has neither intrinsic value nor rights. And I believe this is true whether we are secular philosophers or Christian theologians, whether we speak with the tongues of men or of angels.

III

It is time now to ask what is practically at stake in this disagreement. What are the policy consequences of the biocentrists' position, for which they seek the vocabulary of rights or other strong language? What is denied thereby which would be permitted from the viewpoint of Christian humanism?

Since the biocentrists will not allow us to use nature as we see fit for ourselves, but insist that it has rights or at least claims of its own against us, their general recipe is that it should be left alone wherever possible. There is of course disagreement about the details and the exceptions, but the presumption is in favor of a hands-off policy. That is the *prima facie* rule: let nature take its course. The burden of proof is on us to show why we should be allowed to impose our wills on natural processes.

Concretely this means we should take the necessary measures to protect existing species for their own sakes, not because they might offer something to us in the form of, say, aesthetic pleasure or possible future medicinal benefits. Anthropocentric values must not intrude. Species are to be saved simply because they *are*. The Endangered Species Act should be vigorously defended and enforced; its conflicts with human desires—the spotted owl vs. the timber industry, the snail darter vs. the Tellico Dam—should be settled in favor of the species threatened. The state will have to intervene to protect the species and the land, which means limitations on a landowner's use of his own property. After all, the wild animals and plants on the land should have their freedom, too.

We should especially preserve and expand wild lands, the necessary larger habitats needed for these endangered species, even though humans may desire the land for other purposes, like farming. When it comes to such conflicts, humans ought to lose. Arne Naess, founder of the Deep Ecology school (which is a form of biocentrism tending to argue the equal worth of all natural entities), says with astonishing frankness, "If [human] vital needs come in conflict with the vital needs of nonhumans, then humans should defer to the latter."[31]

We should also leave alone those injured wild creatures whom we are tempted to save—the baby bird fallen from its nest, the wounded animal we come upon in the forest, the whale trapped by the ice. Intervention in natural processes is wrong whether the motives are benevolent or not. The species is strengthened by the premature extinction of its weaker members. Respecting nature's integrity means not imposing our soft-hearted human morality upon it. We should let forest fires burn and have their way with the wild creatures.

We should not build monuments in the wild. No more Mount Rushmores, no Christ of the Andes, no railroads up Mount Washington, and probably no more wilderness roads or ski lifts. We should suspend genetic engineering in agriculture and animal husbandry and not permit there anything we would not permit among humans. We should not take animal lives in teaching biology or medicine, and certainly not in testing cosmetics. Zoos and botanical gardens are suspect; better the species there displayed should live in the wild. We should not keep pets. (There go my Springers.)

What about recreational hunting or fishing? Some biocentrists frown upon it as human interference with nature and unnecessary to our diet besides; but others would permit it as simply a form of predation, which is a fact of nature and not subject to our moral scrutiny. And by this same token there would be no moral obligation for us to become vegetarians. In fact, and rather awkwardly, even plants have a "good of their own" in the biocentric theory, which leads to some mental agility to sort out their permissible uses. It is all right to eat them, of course, for that is nature's way; but "frivolous" uses (Halloween pumpkins? Christmas trees?) are questionable. One suspects that even flower gardening would be a dubious activity, which may be why the biocentric literature rarely (if ever) mentions it.

Although we are in principle to leave nature alone, we are obligated to restore that which we have harmed. This form of intervention is acceptable because it is guided by the principle that pristine nature, before human impact, is somehow ideal. Here again the calculus of permissibility has to be rather finely tuned. It might be wrong to plant trees in a natural desert, for example, but obligatory if human activity had contributed substantially to creating that desert. Obviously this principle can be carried to extremes. Paul Shepherd has seriously suggested that we in this country all move to the coasts and restore the land between to its prehuman condition, in which we would be permitted only as hunter-gatherers, like our most primitive ancestors.[32] Few biocentrists would go anywhere near this far, but the principle is there. The argument is about the moveable boundaries.

My criticism of these limits begins with their vagueness and ambiguity, which is spiced with a generous dash of arbitrariness. Species, we are told, should be allowed to exist until the end of their natural "evolutionary time," but how can we know when that time has arrived? We humans should not take more than our "due" or occupy more than our "fair share" of land or exceed our "limits" in technological grasp; but these terms cannot even begin to be specified. What can be done with any creature turns on its degree of neural complexity, or some other hierarchical principle; but such distinctions will never be clear and are subject to a lot of pure arbitrariness. In the end I suspect that these measures are not in nature, but in ourselves. The lines are drawn according not to objective natural differences but to human preferences: humans supply the values.

The matter of species disappearance is also confused. Leaving nature alone means allowing natural extinctions. Are we then to allow species to vanish, intervening only to save those threatened by human activity? (Yes, says Rolston. New life arises from the old when the demise is natural, but artificial extinction is "without issue."[33]) Or is it our responsibility to preserve as many species as possible no matter what threatens them? Is domestication, far from being harmful interference with the wild, not a useful way to preserve species? In defense of all of us dog owners, I note that many creatures have thrived because of the human presence, mice and rats, famously, and raccoons, and of course all species bred for pets or agricultural utility.

The degree of simplicity of life is another source of confusion. Some biocentrists would allow a fairly complex civilization. Others, like the bioregionalists, would turn their backs on the global economy and live in a locally sustainable way, even reverting to a simple agricultural economy. The movement as a whole can offer us very little real guidance about our permissible impact on the natural world. It would allow us to eat, and to clothe and house ourselves, but require of us some degree of self-limitation because of our exceptional talents, including particularly our talent for reproducing ourselves. But it is very difficult to tell what this directive might mean beyond the generalized complaint that we are too clever and thus exceed our space too readily. We have to pretend we are less, in effect, so that the other creatures may be more; but how and how much are quite unspecifiable.

If we wanted to be a touch perverse, we could point out, as Richard Watson among others has, that leaving nature alone means leaving *Homo Sapiens* alone also, since we are part of nature. The biocentrists are inconsistent in suspending their naturalistic principles in the case of humans. If there is nothing wrong with one species displacing another "naturally," "as has happened millions of times in the history of the Earth," then we humans can do it, too. "To call for curbing man is like trying to make vegetarians out of pet cats." But of course this would be a stupid course if it adversely affected our survival. So we choose our values in our treatment of nature, use our brains, and preserve the kind of environment that will ensure our survival and well-being—a thoroughly anthropocentric activity, and one more logically connected to environmental protection than would be an ascription of inherent value to natural entities. The "normal" and the "natural" in nature are defined by our human interests.[34]

The practical problems with the biocentric theory are many and mainly intractable. They are also mostly unnecessary. Inevitably, once rights for nonhuman entities are proposed, the situation becomes impossibly complex. Absent this proposition, matters become much clearer, though solutions are seldom completely evident. We are still in for a process of experiment, of trial and error, mistake and correction. We have a lot to learn, mostly from science. But with a focus on human welfare we will have a reasonably clear idea how to use our knowledge; the complexities will be simpler, and the conflicts easier to resolve.

It should be added that there is a further desperately serious problem lurking in biocentrism, one which its advocates and critics have debated vigorously. If the focus is on the whole, if the locus of value is primarily ecosystems, or the life process, then the fate of individuals is considerably less important. If the species lives on, it matters little whether particular representatives of it die. Indeed, for the strength and endurance of the species, its weaker members *must* die, lest their enfeebled genes put the whole species at risk.

Most of us will have little difficulty accepting this notion for plants or most insects. Animal rights advocates bitterly contest it for the objects of their concern, as we shall see shortly. When it comes to human beings, we recoil from the implications of this ethic of ecological holism. It is certainly not a theory which will commend itself to Christians, nor should it. It is a cardinal point of our faith that individual human beings are all equally beloved of God, that their lives and well-being should be defended with all our strength, and that any deliberate harm done to them requires the most stringent ethical justification, usually to prevent harm to other humans. The challenge of biocentrism is particularly unsettling at this point, and I shall have to return to it in the final section.

The Animal Rights Distraction

Most people are likely to encounter environmental ethics not in its theological and philosophical guises, fundamental as these surely are, but in one or more popular movements dealing with smaller pieces of the puzzle. Many of these have to do with public policy— pollution controls, waste management, private property rights, and so on. More on these shortly. Two others that generate ethical passion are the ubiquitous animal rights movement, and, less common, but equally captivating and compelling to its adherents, ecofeminism. Both, popular and appealing as they may be to many tastes, turn out on examination to be distractions from a sober environmental ethic.

I

The current power of the movement for animal rights is undeniable. Abetted by the "rights revolution," and by a sometimes difficult marriage to the environmental movement, the old collection of vegetarians and anti-vivisectionists has acquired new vigor. With new power and vigor has come a sizable jump in the temper of the debate. Always sharp-tongued, defenders of animals have increasingly turned to harassing and punitive actions—picketing and boycotting offending businesses, placing lurid ads, raiding and burning laboratories where animal research is conducted, splashing red paint or blood on the houses and cars of the researchers. They are apt to justify their actions in the language of civil disobedience, invoking fidelity to a superior righteousness over the common law.

Public insult has become the order of the day. At best the language of argument is patronizing and contemptuous, at worst downright nasty. Opponents of the movement have been called "vestigial, all who are left over from the cave, who . . . threaten to contaminate the future of mankind . . . with the stink and rot of pain and terror glorified." Mere reform to treat animals better, instead of forswearing their use altogether, "is rather like arguing that the concentration camp at Belsen was more humane than the one at Dachau." Using animals in research is "experimental torture," "as appropriately the study of the half-enlightened man as sport is the amusement of the half-witted." The scientist's joy at discovering knowledge through animal experimentation is "pathological."[35] Nor is the flow of invective all one way. Scorn and ridicule are prominent among the weapons used against the animal rights advocates. Meanness of tone has even invaded scholarly works, well beyond the levels of normal academic waspishness.

It is the presuppositions of the argument which have linked it so closely to the environmental movement, indeed made it the route by which many people have come to environmentalism. If rights are due to creatures other than humans, if a proper ethic requires us to be anti-anthropocentric, then it seemed consistent to go beyond the usual furry and cuddly animals to reptiles and insects, and thence to plants, forests, and ecosystems. It all seemed so clear and simple. In fact it wasn't, and the old allies have fallen apart and exchanged hostile fire. But before we look at the reasons for their separation, let us first examine the original argument for animal rights and find its commonality with environmental ethics.

II

The extent of our concern for animals has seemed to depend, in the first place (before the anthropocentric implications of the reasoning were challenged), on their similarity to or difference from human

37

beings. This subject is a matter of ancient speculation, from Aristotle to Descartes to Darwin and down to the present. Some, like Descartes, have made the difference great, almost absolute; others, like Montaigne, have found it more relative and even slight. Darwin, finely balanced, cites evidence of the immense gap between humans and animals (tool-making, solving mathematical problems, metaphysical reasoning, and disinterested love for all creatures) but also notes similarities (the common possession of senses, emotions, and intuitions like love, memory, attention, curiosity, imitation, even reason).

The stakes in the argument are evident. If animals are quite like us in important respects, then it is easier to claim that they have moral equivalence with us and thus rights against exploitation by us. If they are significantly different, then the bar to their being used by humans is lowered. Peter Singer, a leading spokesman for animal rights, bears, as noted above, the dubious honor of having made popular the term "speciesism" as an epithet to describe those—most of us, he says— who believe the differences are in kind, not just degree. The evocation of and comparison to "racism" is explicit.

> Speciesism is a bare-faced—and morally indefensible—preference for members of our own species . . . exactly the kind of arbitrary difference that the most crude and overt kind of racist uses in attempting to justify racial discrimination. . . . To avoid speciesism we must allow that beings which are similar in all relevant aspects have a similar right to life—and mere membership in our own biological species cannot be a morally relevant criterion for this right.[36]

Those who seek to differentiate animals from humans have often focused on the capacity for language as the distinguishing human characteristic. Descartes argued that even the stupidest man can use language and thus has an adaptive versatility well above even the smartest animal. Here is the famous Cartesian dualism which separates human life, distinctively mental, from the rest of creation, distinctively bodily and mechanistic. Charles Hartshorne, whose interests lie largely with the animal advocates, believes that language is the result of the "symbolic capacity" which distinguishes humans from the other animals, and acknowledges that "[s]ymbolic capacity is our human advantage and superiority. It is a difference in degree so vast that for many purposes one can safely forget that it is one of degree."[37]

Along with language, and of course closely associated with it, the ability to reason is commonly advanced as a uniquely human ability. We have the ability to think out intelligent adaptive responses to unforeseen situations, whereas animals can manage only learned or instinctive responses. Surely the dramatically larger size of the neo-cortex in humans must mark a difference of major significance. Our knowledge of the "mind" or "consciousness" of animals remains scanty, and one must not argue too forcefully from ignorance; but the distinctions which Darwin noted evidently belong to a realm of human capability which animals cannot even approach.[38]

Defenders of animals have naturally sought to minimize the impact of these common-sense assertions. Language is not such a crucial differentiator, they say. Animals have their own sophisticated ways of communicating. Having language is not as great an accomplishment as we think; and even if it were, that would not be an excuse to treat animals as if they were beneath us.[39] Animals' lack of reasoning ability does not really harm the case either. It may be true that we cannot show the presence of animal rationality, but such a lack should not deny to animals their rights and our obligation to respect them. After all, human infants and many mentally defective humans lack qualities which animals may have in greater measure, like intelligence or adaptability; and yet we would not (or most of us would not) deny these humans their rights. Reason, therefore, cannot be made the criterion for distinguishing animal rights from human rights.

This argument from marginal humans is important. Perhaps we may reply that mentally incapacitated people do in fact lose certain rights, although this loss ought to be strictly limited to the exercise of those faculties that have been destroyed by the disease. But they are protected from further loss, from being turned into mere things, available for such use (e.g. medical experimentation) as we may choose, because they are members of a rational species, even though they themselves have "lost their wits." They are afforded generalized protection because they possess, however vestigially, those characteristics that make them human. Protecting them is important to protecting all of us from abuse, should we fall into perilous circumstances, medical, political, or even criminal. Maintaining the human rights even of the insane is a way of defending our species against self-destruction, to say nothing of the fundamental religious reasons many of us would advance for caring for them.

In any event it is clear enough that reason and language do make a major difference in separating animals and humans. The quarrel is over the significance of that distinction.

The most serious and extensive argument for similarity between animals and humans is that concerning sentience, that is, the ability to feel, especially to feel pain. Singer and others are fond of quoting Bentham to the effect that the key question is, "Can they suffer?" If this is accounted the common bond among species, then the implication is clear that pain inflicted on animals must be subject to the same ethical constraints as pain inflicted on humans; for, it is generally assumed, pain is intrinsically evil.

Those who consider animal pain the equivalent of human pain tend to define it as largely a neurological event, an aversive response to bodily assault. The higher animals are also capable of remembering and anticipating such pain in certain contexts, so that aversion to it can be used in behavioral conditioning. Pain in this sense does seem common to humans and animals, which is of course the reason animals are used in pain research.

Whether, as Tom Regan and others claim, "it must then be true that the painful experience of an animal is, considered intrinsically, just as much of an evil as a comparable experience of a human being,"[40] is not quite so obvious. We have no way of comparing the context of such pain, of knowing whether the human capacity to set pain in the context of plans and hopes, for example, makes it a qualitatively different experience from that of animals.[41] Nor can we say with certainty that the neurological event called "pain" is equally evil in all beings who experience it. In any case Regan's simple assertion begs the question we have to answer, which is whether animals and humans have the same moral worth. Without answering that question, we would have to assume it was as evil to hurt a mosquito as to hurt a man—an untenable position which, as we will see in a moment, leads directly to the hierarchical qualification.

It looks very much as if the criterion of sentience, the ability to feel pain, has been chosen *after* the decision to award animals equal moral worth with human beings, chosen to confirm a position already taken. We may infer as much from the way Regan and Joel Feinberg qualify their use of the sentience factor. Feinberg believes it prohibits "behavior that inflicts *unnecessary* pain or torment on a creature capable of suffering—that is, pain for which there is no good or sufficient reason." Regan thinks that the presence of sentience means that "causing pain is always *prima facie* wrong," i.e. wrong unless there is some overriding human good. Thus for both men the sentience principle in the end does not establish full moral equality between animals and humans, for both of them would permit animal pain for clear human benefit. Indeed, precisely because sentience turns out to be so inadequate a safeguard for animal rights, Regan later abandons it for the claim that animals possess an "inherent value" that does *not* depend solely on the ability to feel pain. It does seem clear that sentience was chosen to confirm a prior position rather than itself being the fact that forced the conclusion. And if that is so, then we may equally arbitrarily select some other criteria for determining rights, and do so with the intent of confining rights to humans. R. G. Frey suggests, for example, the capacity to experience beauty, or the possession of free will and moral agency, both of which would exclude animals.[42] (The biocentrists, with an entirely different goal, cannot use sentience because it will not protect plants or ecosystems. Here again, the intent determines the criterion, and they find other qualities which will award rights to nature.)

I believe, however, that it is dangerous to link rights to properties, lest we find ourselves excluding impaired human beings from the rights community. Most animal advocates, on the contrary, do try to link rights to qualities or properties, capacities which they then argue are common to humans and animals. The result is anthropomorphism, sometimes called the "pathetic fallacy," and the literature of animal rights advocacy is full of it. As a bumper sticker of the Humane Society puts it, "Animals are small people in furry coats."

III

One of the most obvious common sense challenges to animal rights advocates is to ask whether they mean seriously to equate the moral standing of humans and, say, insects or plants? And if they do not, where, they might be asked, is their personal cut-off line, and why was it chosen? Perhaps surprisingly, in view of their initial claim to be placing animals, or all sentient life, in the same moral community with humanity, many retreat to some kind of hierarchical view— very much like the way biocentrists solve *their* problem of conflicting rights—distinguishing among different life forms, awarding privileges and protection to some that they would deny to others.

There is no consensus on the criteria, though a popular choice is the degree of neurological development. Hartshorne would place humans and animals above trees, because the former have a nervous system. Cutting a tree, then, is "not analogous to killing a deer or even a fish." But he would award stronger rights to horses and apes than to human embryos, precisely because the latter have nervous systems functioning at a much lower level.[43]

Regan accepts a hierarchy that permits him to kill lower forms of life but not mammals, the cut-off point obviously a matter of neurological development: "There is no rational basis for believing that anything we do to cancer cells matters to these cells themselves, or that it makes a difference to their quality of life as experienced by them, or, in short, that they can be benefited or harmed by what we do to them."[44]

Comparisons like these, which are at the extremes, from, as it were, opposite ends of the continuum of life, are relatively easy. The hard choices lie in the middle. Singer accepts this challenge and draws a precise line: if a being can't suffer or enjoy, then "there is nothing left to take into account," and we may, for example, eat it. There is an "evolutionary scale," and as we descend it, these capacities diminish. He would include fish and reptiles within the protected sphere, because they can suffer. He would also protect crustaceans, but mollusks seem so primitive that it is "difficult to imagine them feeling pain, or having other mental states."[45] And that is where he would draw the line: between shrimp and clams.

Other writers make similar distinctions with more or less precision, all accepting some hierarchical solution to the moral challenge. Feinberg's criterion, making him one of the most moderate of animal defenders, is "level of rational awareness," which means that "the animal 'right to life,' if there is such a thing, is generally held to be a much weaker claim than its human counterpart." John Cobb's hierarchy is based on evolutionary development, with "consciousness" as the highest state, ascribed to all the animal kingdom. There is value, he thinks, in the unconscious experience of simple animals, plants, even electrons (the process philosophers can descend the great chain of being further than anyone else); but he ranks all experience by its quantity and complexity in such a way that human happiness and misery are more important than that of other creatures. He claims to be going "beyond anthropocentrism," and yet, anthropocentrically in spite of himself, puts man at the apex of his value pyramid.[46]

Clark, annoyed at the "hierarchically inclined," is hardly less so himself: "Is it really supposed that microorganisms have as developed a point of view as such complex creatures as squids [who incidentally are mollusks] and cows and cats?" Further, "I hold no special brief for cockroaches, and am prepared to believe that their sentience is of another order than mine, or than a monkey's."[47]

Although this hierarchical thinking is typical of animal defenders, there are also radicals among them who are quite contemptuous of what they see as a fatal compromise with the anthropocentrists. And just as is the case with the radical biocentrists, they look to Albert Schweitzer as one of their heroes. Schweitzer would protect, or at least have "reverence" for all life of any kind, even insects and plants. He would pluck no leaf from a tree, nor allow bugs to fly into his lamp and be killed. He would pick up worms stranded on the pavement and place them on the grass. From sheer necessity he would mow a field to make fodder for cows, but not cut even a flower unnecessarily. As a medical doctor he tolerated animal experimentation, but only if absolutely necessary, and even then at the price of guilt which had to be recompensed by treating other animals and insects with great reverence.[48]

Before the biocentrists came along, the idea of giving plants equal rights with animals, because clear moral lines could not be drawn between them, might easily have reduced the animal rights movement to absurdity. We would have a "plant liberation movement" accompanied by disdainful laughter. But, as we have seen, the biocentrists took up the argument and extended the animal rights movement to its logical conclusion: plants do have rights, as all life does. Animal advocates were tempted to go along with this "extension," but were also reluctant. Regan allows that plants might indeed have rights, even if they weren't aware of their own interests. Even things which can't know their own good can have rights, so it wouldn't be necessary to postulate "contented broccoli" to make this claim. Feinberg, on the other hand, would not award rights to plants and "mere things" because, unlike animals, they cannot experience suffering and frustration. Singer, using the sentiency criterion, also draws the moral line between plants and animals, and so has no trouble using plants as he wishes: "There is no reliable evidence that plants are capable of feeling pleasure or pain." Raising the issue of plants' rights is an obfuscatory device by people whose main purpose is to undermine vegetarianism.[49]

Here we can see the eventual quarrel between the animal advocates and the biocentrists in its early stages. As the argument over rights developed, their differences became irreconcilable, fully justifying the blunt title of Mark Sagoffs' article, "Animal Liberation and Environmental Ethics: Bad Marriage, Quick Divorce."[50]

The difficulty lies principally in deciding who, or what, has rights. Animal advocates, who consider animals as similar to humans in all morally relevant respects, normally view rights on the model of human rights. In that respect their view might even be considered an extended anthropocentrism. Just as we would defend all humans, even the impaired, so we should protect all animals. The theory is *individualistic*. Basic rights, like life, freedom, and being spared unnecessary suffering, are meaningless if they do not apply to each and every individual. Biocentrists, however, give priority to species. Their ethic is *holistic*. Indifferent to suffering in the wild (just part of the natural ecosystem, which is good), they would allow, even encourage, the death of weaker individuals so that the species as a whole may flourish. It is the life *process*, the entire system, that must concern us ethically, which is why species count and the individuals in them do not.

For this position the animal rights advocates can hardly forgive them. In a now famous reaction Tom Regan fastened upon biocentrism the charming sobriquet "ecofascism." But biocentrists reject the "humanitarian ethic" as misplaced in nature. It is not a true "environmental ethic." Rolston, who would allow hunting and fishing, considers the ethic of the wild to be different from that of culture (with disturbing qualifications, as we shall see), and that we are to conform to the former in treating wild creatures. We should not be troubled if a wolf kills other wild animals, but if it invades the sphere of culture by killing domestic cattle, we may in turn kill the wolf. He notes that in the story of Noah's ark, the point, the divine priority, is to save the *species* by rescuing breeding pairs. Individuals are left to perish. Hear also Sagoff memorably separating environmental ethics from humanitarianism: "Mother Nature is so cruel to her children she makes Frank Perdue look like a saint."[51]

There have been attempts at mediating this quarrel. Lawrence Johnson's proposal for saving the marriage turns on his grounding of rights not in qualities but in interests. All living things, he says, have a "good" or interest determined by what they are by nature. Thus their resemblance to humans, or lack of it, is not relevant, and we can defend the rights of individual animals and trees with comparable fervor. However, the scale of values that he employs to solve conflicts of rights is weighted in favor of species. All interests may count, but they do not count equally; and species, which are more important for the functioning of the entire biosphere, count more than individuals. A species, in fact, is not a collection or class of individuals, but a thing in itself, with well-being and interests, especially in survival; and we humans must honor this interest even at considerable cost to ourselves.[52] Given this clear priority, Johnson's effort is not likely to satisfy traditional animal advocates. I suspect they are more likely to think he belongs, however kind his intentions, however sincere his appreciation of animals' worth, among the "ecofascists."

IV

In the end, after the smoke of battle has cleared, we can see not only that the animal rights movement contributes little to environmental ethics, but that it cannot really make a convincing case for those rights at all. Claims for the similarity between animals and humans can as easily be replaced by arguments for great differences. The sentience criterion is arbitrary. The claim that having a good of one's own confers rights is simply not true, for the good of some entities is distinctly inimical to other forms of life. Interests do not automatically produce rights: we have an interest in not having our feelings hurt, for example, but no consequent right to be spared criticism. Animal rights advocates cannot even agree on the content of the rights they advocate, some allowing what others would forbid, e.g. eating meat, using animals in experiments, and in general prescribing widely different degrees of stringency. And this collective inability to reach some kind of consensus suggests the weakness of their basic claim.

Among human beings, rights imply reciprocal obligations or responsibilities. This is not true for animals, who can't make promises or contracts and don't show any inter-species obligations. If they did, there would be no predatory relations. Animals aren't able to be "guilty" in any sense. Dogs can only be called "bad" (with the appropriate tone of voice) because they are trained to expect reproach for behaving in certain ways. Their training is based on conditioning. Animals are not moral agents and cannot, for example, be held criminally responsible for their acts, which is why we laugh at those occasional medieval attempts to try animals in court.[53] Some animal advocates counter that this lack of responsibility doesn't disqualify them as holders of rights, even if they can't return the favor. Human babies, after all, have rights but no responsibilities. But this is again the argument from marginal humans; and my answer is, to state it once more, that babies have rights because they are only "defective" (or incomplete) members of the species to which rights belong.

Sometimes animal rights defenders, dissatisfied with their own arguments, retreat to the simple assertion that animals possess "inherent" rights simply because they exist, because they are living creatures and all living creatures have rights. This is an argument they have in common with the biocentrists. Regan argues that inherent value means that animals or trees or people are subjects of a life that is of value to them whether or not it is good or useful to anyone else. But this is scarcely different from the interests argument, as we see when he argues that a "good car" can be good whether or not we value it. Most of us would argue that what makes a car good is properties which appeal to a human driver. Regan also argues similarly that plants have value in themselves because they can die, but few of us would read rights into this fact.[54] Interests, to repeat, do not confer rights.

Once again, as was the case with the biocentrists, we find ourselves in impossible contradictions when we try to extend the concept of rights beyond the human community. A sober Christian humanism—call it anthropocentrism if you wish—avoids these crippling entanglements. We do not really know anything about animal rights; the term is meaningless to us. Value terms like rights cannot be weighed between species that cannot communicate. That is why we are left scratching our heads at comments like that of James Rachels, that when a big bird drives a small one out of the nest, or when a cat eats a mouse, we recognize that as an injustice, even though the animals in question couldn't possibly understand what justice was.[55]

Why does this statement puzzle us so? Because it is anthropomorphizing, applying to animals a human concept, justice, that is entirely inappropriate in the animal world. It belongs to intra-human speech only. To some extent we all speak that way of animals, especially our pets; but we know, if we reflect on what we are saying, that we are speaking only in metaphor. I say my dogs are "jealous" of each other in competing for my affection, but of course I have no way of knowing what emotion they do experience.

If the arguments for animal rights all fail, as I think they do, what principles, then, should govern our treatment of animals? Are there no limits if they have no rights? What is consistent with a Christian humanistic approach to ethics? There no doubt are limits, but they derive only from a realistic anthropocentrism and inhere in decisions about what is useful and valuable to humanity. One such limit arises from human mercy, charity, sympathy. We treat animals kindly as a reflection of our own natures, not giving in to cruel or angry impulses. Our treatment reflects the kind of people we are, and if we think about it, the kind of people we would like to be. There may well be, as many distinguished thinkers including St. Thomas, Locke, and Kant have argued, a link between the way we treat animals and the way we treat human beings; and kind treatment of animals thus has an indirect "spillover" effect in promoting a kinder, gentler society.

Besides sympathy there is also our compelling religious restraint, that we are given charge over the rest of creation to manage it responsibly for its maker and true owner. This is, again, the principle of stewardship, and it clearly implies limits to what we may do with animals as with anything else. It certainly forbids cruelty and wanton destruction, and, more positively, enjoins active care. Perhaps it may be said that our duties toward animals as God's creatures imply that they have a kind of "right" in a soft sense; but I think it is better, clearer, to express this obligation as stewardship than to confuse it with the language of rights, which belongs to an entirely different, human context.

V

I might add, postscriptively as it were, that this human-centered view of the status of animals has certain obvious practical consequences and provides solutions to many current controversies.

The Status of Wild Animals

Animal rights advocates would close the zoos, because animals should be free, not caged, as a consequence of their rights. But, rejecting the argument for animal rights and reasoning anthropocentrically, I would keep the zoos open. They are for human education

47

and enjoyment, do no frivolous harm to animals, and serve the conservationist purpose of protecting animals from harm, even extinction. Like wildlife management in general, zoos reflect the principle of good stewardship and are a fine expression of our human responsibility for the rest of creation. I would also acknowledge frankly that we may kill animals that disserve our interests, e.g. insect pests, the course of appropriate action being determined mostly by good ecological science.

Domestic Animals

If animals do have rights, then work animals and pets are simply slaves. But since, as I argue, they don't have rights, a permissible anthropocentrism allows us to breed and keep animals for work or our pleasure, as long as they are kindly treated. That is, the controlling limit is sympathy, not rights.

Eating Meat

The vegetarian argument is that if animals have rights, then eating them is the moral equivalent of cannibalism; and killing them, especially killing them painfully, is a crime. Furthermore, not eating meat is better for our health and, given the amount of grain the domestic herds consume, an inefficient and wasteful way to produce food. But, we may reply, if animals are not the moral equivalent of humans, then breeding them for food is acceptable. The principle of kind treatment should, however, impel us to make certain regulations governing the conditions of animals raised for slaughter. As for the ecological and nutritional arguments against meat eating, these are of a different order and have whatever standing they have independent of whether animals are ethically available for our use.

Scientific Research

Driven by a mixture of motives—identification with the helplessness of victims, suspicion of modern technological medicine, a sympathy for alternative therapies like homeopathic medicine, even acceptance of illness and early death and a refusal to combat it—many activists oppose altogether the use of animals for research. They would have us use instead tissue cultures or computer models, or, failing that, forswear knowledge gained so wrongfully. In using laboratory animals we are no better than Nazis experimenting on people. Better we should die than fall into such sin. It is, after all, precisely the similarity of animals to humans that makes them good research subjects for humans. Hence the researcher's paradox: The more animals are like us, the more they are useful in research, and the less available they are ethically for that research.

A practical, sober anthropocentrism, of course, not only permits but *requires* our use of laboratory animals. The benefits to humanity have been enormous, and could not have been obtained by cell cultures or computers. Research with animals has gone a long way toward saving us from illness and misery. Anti-scientific romanticism is a luxury of the comfortable—and the healthy. I would permit some restraints, based on the kindness principle, perhaps in such areas as using animals in product testing, though reform of insurance and tort laws might be more useful. In any case, drawing the ethical line firmly between humans and nonhuman animals saves the research enterprise, negates the Nazi example, and protects human rights.

Sport and Fashion

Hunting and fishing, say the animal rights advocates, are impermissible because they inflict pain for mere sport. The argument that natural death in the wild is more painful than by gunshot or fisherman's knife, that the population of wild creatures not taken by sportsmen will be left to the cruelties of starvation, does not impress these people. Some of their literature against hunting is also thinly disguised class contempt, or hatred of males.[56] They are also critical of the use of animals for clothing or fashion, and for the same ultimate reason: animals' rights are violated. But if we do not accept animal rights, we need have no more objection to the use of animals for clothing than for food. The kindness limit might impose some restraints on hunting, but there is no reason to suppose that sportsmen are insincere in thinking they do more good than harm to wild populations as a whole.

These examples are meant to suggest how reasonable might be the resolution of current issues in animal welfare if we take stewardship and kindness as our guides and reject the crippling, anti-humanistic tangles of the animal rights movement. To be as modest as a forthright anthropocentrism dictates, let us conclude simply that the movement has not made a compelling case for animal rights, nor for a legitimate place in a proper environmental ethic.

49

The Ecofeminist Distraction

Mention "ecofeminism" and most people will say they have never heard of it. To the uninitiated the word rings oddly. But with a little explanation it generates a lively curiosity, and slowly it is forcing its way into the ecological consciousness of everywoman, and, less inexorably, everyman. References to it are steadily increasing; anthologies dealing with "deep ecology" or "radical ecology" regularly include essays on it. In some form it is perhaps the inevitable result of the meeting of ecology and feminism, two of the most powerful movements of our time. It has, moreover, a certain ecumenicity, adaptable to a variety of interests. Part serious exercise in the history of ideas, part political activism, and part "new-age spirituality," it has the power to attract or repel many different kinds of people for many different reasons.

I

Ecofeminist writers are as varied as their subject. Some are full-time academics, often in Women's Studies departments. Some are part-timers who "teach classes" on Goddess worship, Native American lore, humanistic psychology, "witchcraft," "shamanism," and the like. Many are politically active in environmental issues, women's health concerns, or animal rights. There are women who live "simply and ecologically," directors of institutes of various sorts, new-age types (e.g. "an elder who nurtures life on earth," or a "midwife, healer, and spiritual dancer"), facilitators, poets, and essayists who write everything from thoughtful analyses to intemperate rants. They are also, not surprisingly, overwhelmingly women.

What ties all these elements together and justifies giving them a single name is the shared conviction that the root cause of our many crises is a devaluation of natural processes produced by a thoroughly inimical masculine consciousness. The ubiquitous "patriarchy," driven by an attitude of dominance and oppression, seeks to gain control over women, over nature, and for that matter over other people, male and female alike. Virtually all of our social problems—militarism, agricultural decline, educational inadequacy, poverty, greedy capitalism, heedless industrialism, the inferior status of women, environmental deterioration, and more—are caused by men, not women, and will not yield until we have a worldwide basic conversion—to ecofeminism.

The vision is sweeping, astonishing, audacious, even a touch messianic. The conversion required is so fundamental, so ultimate, it deserves to be called religious. Or, to put it in secular terms, we require (what else?) a "paradigm shift," every crisis-monger's current cliché.

What makes this triumphalist feminism particularly *ecological* feminism is the conviction that women are in some way closer to nature than men and are despised and oppressed by men precisely for that reason. The subjugation of nature and women is of one essence. "Male domination of women and domination of nature are interconnected, both in cultural ideology and in social structures." "The logic of domination has functioned historically within patriarchy to sustain and justify the twin dominations of women and nature." Put nastily, the violence of men toward women and toward nature is one and the same. "The hatred of women and the hatred of nature are intimately connected and mutually reinforcing." To sexism, racism, ageism, classism, and so on, one must add "naturism," all oppressions with a single root in the masculine concept of dominance.[57]

Thus the deliverance of women from male oppression is at the same time inevitably the rescue of nature from despoliation. And this is true no matter what the particular ecological problem. All of them—pollution, soil erosion, hunger, global warming, over-grazing, deforestation, loss of the rain forest, growth of deserts, disappearance of species, the mistreatment of animals, even AIDS—will yield only when patriarchy has been overthrown.

In accepting and celebrating the idea that women are indeed closer to nature than men, ecofeminism parts company with what may be called "liberal feminism." The interest of the latter is in women's equality with men, in equal opportunity, equal pay, equal rights. Liberal feminists want to be integrated fully into mainstream "male" culture and have no intention of letting ecology become isolated as a female issue. In fact, associating women especially with nature is and always has been a disaster for women, forming the very basis of their oppression, ensuring their permanent marginalization, confining them to the role of nurturers. If there is one idea that the feminist movement in all its parts has heretofore seemed to agree on, it is that "biology is *not* destiny."

But against this feminist orthodoxy ecofeminists sin boldly. Women's special tie to nature is assured by their biological role in giving birth and nursing the young. The facts of reproductive biology

51

dominate a woman's life much more than a man's. Her experience of nature is clearly different from his. This difference is literally essential, that is, it belongs to the essence of womanhood. Woman, like nature "herself," is in essence the nurturing mother. The female difference must be the occasion not for subordination but for superiority. Ecofeminists mean to reverse what they see as an ancient history of devaluation and instead claim that women are better, healthier, precisely because they are more connected to nature, more natural. The ecologically sound society of the future must therefore be a "female" culture, the obverse of the destructive "male" culture we now have.

The ecofeminist movement is sufficiently diverse, however, that not all participants are willing to accept this essentialist doctrine which bifurcates the human race so completely. It may well be that women, because of their nature and their relative powerlessness in contemporary industrial society, are better positioned than men to lead us into a healthy ecological future. But their roles have also been constructed socially and culturally, not wholly dependent on biological differences. Women are fully human also, after all, and like men participate in the transcendence of nature, if in a different and perhaps lesser way. One of the essential tasks of civilization, for example, is the socializing of children, and this has been primarily the domain of women. It may be that women are in an intermediate role between nature and culture (as Sherry Ortner argues),[58] and from that position, not from total immersion in nature, are best situated to lead the way to a healthier future.

So there are cautionary voices which fear that the movement might once again entrap women in inferior roles. But ecofeminists are at one in their general belief that women know more of nature than men, that women ought not and cannot aspire to have a life like that of men, who are alienated from nature in their quest for the goods of the mind, of transcendent spirit.

Inevitably the premises of ecofeminism lead to hostility toward men, so widespread and generalized that it deserves to be called sexism. "It is . . . the numbing of our innate human sensibilities that makes it possible for men to dominate, oppress, exploit, and kill." "Cut out of . . . the process of birth and child-rearing, . . . men become monstrous and crazed." "Males . . . project onto women their own rejection of their 'lower selves,'" and it is "the bottomless void of male insecurity" which now "brings human society to the brink of annihilation." "The patriarchal outrages" include "racism, harassment of homosexuals, increasing violence against women, forced prostitution, pornography, non-personhood for women . . . , economic oppression, and nuclear power and weaponry," all the result of "the immensely destructive thrashing of patriarchal leaders who cannot even name the pain and ignorance that drive their greed." This villainous patriarchy, in Rosemary Ruether's wonderfully excited prose, has produced "a million women twisted on the rack, smoldered in burning faggots to pay homage to [their] Lie," and desiring a future where "Enlightened man . . . will mount upon [the cosmos] with wings, fly away to the moon, blow her up in a flash of atomic energy, live forever in a space capsule, entombed in plastic, dining on chemicals."[59]

Predictably and unfortunately, the overuse of the word "rape" is a staple of ecofeminist writing. "The physical rape of women by men in this culture is easily paralleled by our rapacious attitude toward the Earth itself. She, too is female." "The rape of the earth becomes a metaphor for the rape of women," and "when we resist the rape of the earth, we are fighting the same mentality that resists the rape of women."[60]

Some ecofeminists wish to narrow the generic sexism of their movement and target only *white* males, or even more narrowly white, Western, economically privileged males. "The ecological crisis is related to the systems of hatred of all that is natural and female by the white, Western male formulations . . . the systematic denigration of working-class people and people of color, women, and animals."[61] This move avoids the obvious difficulty of numbering poor men in poor countries among the world's oppressors (though domestic violence there may be another matter). It also has the utility of confining one's venom to the only politically acceptable villains left, white, Western males. But it also suggests an awkward problem, the status of privileged white Western *women*, who may very well appear to non-Western people of color, men and women alike, to be more part of the problem than part of the answer. Ecofeminists tend to avoid this inconsistency in their argument, though some do acknowledge its existence. Again, there are other voices, not as extreme, who hope for some sort of new partnership between the sexes, a complementarity which will not despise men. But one must report honestly that these moderate voices are a minority.

II

Beyond the generalized gender abuse of the movement there is a specific charge aimed at the way men think, or are alleged to think, a charge which is nothing less than an attack on the foundations of Western science. Men, it is said, have a penchant for reason, for objectifying, distancing, analyzing, thus seeking not only to know but also to control and dominate. These are habits of thought which they apply not only to the material world but also to other people, and especially to women. The discovery of nature's secrets by scientific experimentation results from the same mind-set as subjugating and exploiting women, who, of course, are part of nature in a way that men are not. Moreover, the language of experimentation is "bold sexual imagery: . . . hard facts, penetrating mind, . . . the thrust of his argument," which of course shows the mentality of the masculine rapist at work, with nature and women as his victims. "Sexual politics helped to structure the nature of the empirical method."[62]

And so one must reject the masculine "left-brained" way of thinking, the "dominant white male western rationality . . . based on linear, dichotomized thought patterns that divide reality into dualism: . . . good and . . . bad, superior and inferior, domin[ant] and suppressed."[63] Thus do the heroes of Western science—the Bacons, Descartes, and Newtons—become re-minted as villains.

To replace this mechanistic model of nature ecofeminists offer us their "organic" or "organismic" model. Women think differently, with "the voice of the heart, love, conscience, unconsciousness, compassion, sensitivity, sensuality, nature, nonlinear intuitive perception." Their principal values are "care, love, friendship, trust, and appropriate reciprocity." Instead of the male stress on competition and exploitation, women want cooperation; instead of rationality, they use intuition. We must cooperate with nature rather than seek to control it, or "her." If nature were seen as a living organism instead of dead matter, it would not be so harmfully treated. Without the baneful influence of Newtonian physics, we would not have so much "intellectual arrogance toward nature." Nor would we treat each other so badly. Feminine thought would restore moral community, a sense of interconnectedness and mutual responsibility among people. In short, for a viable future, with nature and among peoples, we must return to a pre-scientific organic worldview.[64]

The "organismic" community involves a specific rejection of

anthropocentrism. "An ecological-feminist theology of nature . . .
must question the hierarchy of human over nonhuman nature." We
must not concentrate our moral attention on human beings, but
include within the circle of our concern, as equal partners, all living
things, all animals, indeed the whole natural world. Our goal should
be "equity between the human species and all other members of the
biotic community of which we are a part." All species have "intrinsic
value," value which does not depend on their usefulness to human
beings. "There is no hierarchy in nature: among persons, between
persons and the rest of the natural world, or among the many forms
of nonhuman nature." "We must respond to a 'thou-ness' in all
beings."[65]

At this point very much like biocentrism, ecofeminism also joins
the biocentric critique of the Western religious tradition, objecting to
the idea that we are made "in the image of God" to exercise stewardship over the earth. Thinking of ourselves as special deludes us into
believing we have a right to dominate nature; and stewardship
inevitably implies that we are superior to the rest of the natural
world, that sound environmental policy is a case of *noblesse oblige*,
"the homocentric ethics of ecosystem management."[66]

III

This train of thought culminates in an embrace of the "Gaia hypothesis" of James Lovelock, the idea that the earth is alive like a living
person whom we may name after the ancient Greek goddess of the
earth. The earth behaves like a unified organism and takes on the
attributes of genuine divinity. Here we have a species of theological
immanentism, but with a specific feminist twist: the divine principle
has "female" attributes, and is called "Goddess" to make the point.

"She" is best celebrated in appropriately female rites. Worship
embraces "the sacred link between the Goddess in her many guises
and totemic animals and plants, sacred groves, and womblike caves,
in the moon-rhythm blood of menses, the ecstatic dance."[67] Peter
Berger has remarked that ecofeminism here represents the irruption
into our modern lives of the "mythological matrix," where the
boundaries between the worlds of humans, nature, and gods are
fluid and permeable. And this same mythological mind, so characteristic of archaic societies, is ever with us, as students of popular
religiosity well know.

Of course since such imagery belongs to a pre-scientific, archaic worldview, its actual rituals are largely lost and unrecoverable. But ecofeminists are not shy about inventing new rituals which they think evocative of the mythic past, even though inevitably such an invented religion suffers from a certain lack of authenticity. The favored attributes of the "Goddess" turn out to be those congruent with the contemporary ecofeminist political program: egalitarian, sharing, giving images, but also strong and creative ones, images which validate the worshipers as female, made "in the image of the Goddess." This religious program "will help to bring the attitudes and feelings of the deep mind into harmony with feminist social and political goals, and reciprocally . . . will express and bring to articulation the feminist intuition that the struggle for equal rights is supported by the nature of reality."[68]

Perhaps to neutralize the elements of deliberate self-serving invention in ecofeminist religious rites, many writers have sought to ground their theological desires in forms of Goddess worship which are not only authentic but available for study and emulation. That search has led them to resources like the many Goddesses of contemporary Hinduism, or some of the still-extant rites of Native Americans, or to what is reasonably knowable about some of the cults of ancient Egypt or Greece, the adoration of Goddesses who have strength, creativity, and explicit female sexuality, sometimes quite unbridled.

Unfortunately these real Goddesses have another side, not only creative and nurturing and fertile, but a side of death and destruction, terrifying, merciless, demonic. But their modern advocates profess not to be put off by this dark side, rather to regard this inversion of value as realism and its incorporation into divinity as healthy. In the Goddess what we perceive as evil is incarnated and then transcended, "destroying the finite to reveal the infinite."[69]

With all the problems attendant on real Goddess cults, it has seemed better to many ecofeminists to posit an archaic utopia where the religion of the Goddess really did prevail and where none of the difficulties of the historically available cults existed. One might then hope to recover this ancient perfection, since, the argument goes, it really did once exist. Shreds of archaeological evidence—an unearthed female statuette here and there, for example—are offered as proof, along with the (rather presumptuous) claim that the mere existence of myths of the golden age of the Goddess show that there really was such a period.

It was supposedly a time of harmony between the sexes, dominated by the female values of "caring, compassion, and non-violence," not the masculine ones of "conquest and domination." "Peaceful and progressive societies thrived for millennia where gynocentric values prevailed."[70] But, the story goes, this paradise was destroyed by the conquest of fierce horsemen from elsewhere (the Asian steppes, perhaps) who imposed their masculine sky God, full of fire and violence, and drove the peaceable Earth Mother underground (an ironically fitting fate). Henceforth the "patriarchy" has ruled, to our everlasting harm. It is long past time to return to what we have lost, to appropriate the ancient Goddess worship for today and bring back the peaceable kingdom.

Unfortunately for this revision of the myth of the fall from Eden, the evidence for such a golden age is slim to nonexistent. Feminists who for ideological reasons wish to find bygone matriarchies as a justification for empowering women today will be hard-pressed to offer credible documentation of their thesis, says Joan Bamberger. Sherry Ortner is equally blunt: "I would flatly assert that we find women subordinated to men in every known society. The search for a genuinely egalitarian, let alone matriarchal, culture has proved fruitless."[71]

Other writers who locate themselves in the ecofeminist movement, like Ynestra King and Rosemary Ruether, are equally critical of this romantic, ideologically driven search for an unknowable past. Far from returning to prehistory, "We thoughtful human beings must use the fullness of our sensibility and intelligence to push ourselves intentionally to another stage of evolution," a stage of "rational reenchantment" where the intuitive and scientific, the mystical and rational, are fused in a new way of being.[72] There is little point in trying to defend the indefensible, and the myth of matriarchy doesn't contribute to women's emancipation in any case. It is more to the point to note that images of the divine in cultures ancient and modern show both male and female attributes, that the nature of ultimate reality must reflect a wholeness which includes both masculine and feminine qualities.

Still, Goddess-worshiping neopaganism has considerable popularity in the ecofeminist mainstream, where its enunciation is invariably accompanied by a rejection of Western monotheism, held to represent the dominance of the patriarchal sky God. This masculine God is the antithesis of the earth Goddess, and thus the antithesis of

ecological wisdom. Instead of the nature-loving earthbound immanent deity, the monotheistic God of the cosmos encourages a "radical
disesteem for the Earth, that insignificant and lowly region we
inhabit."[73] And, reflecting the intimate association of nature with the
female, the God of Western monotheism also devalues women,
denigrating the body in favor of the spirit, a characteristically masculine enterprise.

What, then, is to be done with the major religious traditions of
the West? The answer for a significant sector of the ecofeminist
movement, and perhaps its majority, is to reject those traditions
altogether. The rejectionists, like Carol Christ, would discard the
Western tradition as hopelessly sexist and call for the reemergence
of the Goddess, an image of the transcendent divinity which would
revalue women and nature. Or perhaps we should have again a
frank pagan polytheism, not even a "Goddess monotheism."[74]

There are, however, those whose affection for the tradition remains strong despite their commitment to ecofeminism, and who
believe they can find what they need in heretofore under-emphasized
themes of Christianity and Judaism. Thus Rosemary Ruether, searching through the Christian tradition, constructs a synthesis to her
liking, blending a "cosmological Christology" (Christ as the wisdom
of God immanent in the whole cosmos, following Matthew Fox), the
participation of nature in the drama of salvation (the mind insepara-
ble from matter, following Teilhard de Chardin) and the "process
theology" of A. N. Whitehead and his school, where all entities, even
matter, have mentality and can decline the options posed by the God
who "lures" beings into an optimal future.[75]

Many variations on these themes are possible, obviously. The
choice is not simply posed between rescue of the Western tradition
and flight to neopaganism, but includes all manner of subtleties
between. There is some sentiment for Eastern religions, too, although
there is also ecofeminist criticism of this religious family for encouraging a detached spirituality indifferent to avoidable human suffering, or promoting a loss of the good of individuals in some kind of
"whole," much like the generic fault of biocentrism—although the
fault really extends to much of ecofeminism also.

IV

Not surprisingly the ecofeminist vision as described thus far is, with
some notable exceptions, hostile to technology. Patriarchal nature-

conquering science and technology is the source of our ecological troubles, the masculine mind run rampant, evil exploitation unbound. A special subset of this Luddite anger is directed at modern medicine, triumphant over traditional herbal-based medicine largely administered by women and based on the healing power of nature. Technological medicine is another way that men exercise power and control over nature and women.

Ecofeminism's alternatives to technological society include efforts to live in a more or less self-sustaining manner in small areas, in harmony with the land. Economies need to be decentralized to promote local autonomy. This program is of course set against the emerging economic interdependence of nations, the so-called global economy.

With occasional embarrassment and some muting of the point, ecofeminism in general—and again with exceptions—is equally unenthusiastic about third world development. The natural rural economy of subsistence, in which women play a dominant role, is not the bad system it has been pictured to be, but a way of living in an ecologically sound and harmonious way without being dependent on and controlled by distant centers of power. Development actually hurts people's ability to subsist and increases their real material poverty. So, "throughout the third world, women, peasants, and tribals are struggling for liberation from 'development' just as they earlier struggled for liberation from colonialism."[76]

Romanticizing peasant and tribal cultures is, however, not to everyone's taste, not even among ecofeminists. These "indigenous peoples" have themselves committed many ecological sins and are hardly models of peace and sexual equality. They really do live in material poverty, and to withhold technology from them by idealizing primitive life is to condemn them to misery. Technology itself is not the problem: it is "integral to the human condition, . . . part of the evolutionary impulse, the striving for the expansion of our potential as human beings." It is rather the use to which technology is put, in the service of masculine domination, that is the difficulty.[77]

The danger for ecofeminists in opposing technology and development is that this resistance compromises their desire to be on the side of people they deem oppressed, including not only the third world but also women and working-class people everywhere. There is an inherent tension in the movement between this desire and their fundamental premise that natural ecosystems are hurt by modern human economic activity, a tension that is often papered over by the flat assertion, without much defense or explanation, that justice among peoples is dependent on the well-being of the earth. "The goals of feminism, ecology, and movements against racism and for the survival of indigenous peoples are internally related. . . ."[78] Eco-feminism embraces here the concept of "eco-justice" which we shall revisit in the next section.

V

The ecofeminist movement has many faults—what interesting movement does not?—but some seem particularly crippling or disabling. Its initial and most general proposition, that all crises are bound together by one theme of patriarchalism and solvable by one antidote, the ecofeminist conversion, is itself highly suspect. Practical wisdom tells us that social problems are of different sorts, yield to different solutions, and can really be solved piecemeal: one thinks of the dramatic improvement since the expiration of the cold war in the once all-dominating problem of nuclear annihilation. There is a naive utopianism in the conviction that all evils will be eradicated with the triumph of a new ideology—a hauntingly familiar error here dressed up in new language.

Nor is the specific identification of women with nature as a unity, opposed to men, altogether plausible, even though the movement regards this dichotomy as unarguable. Liberal feminists are probably correct to reject this dangerous gambit, which appears to make women subhuman. Women are not more drawn to ecological concern than men, and the "conjunction"[79] of the women's movement with the environmental movement is no more than that: a fortuitous conjunction, not causative. It is always tempting to regard events occurring at the same time as internally united, even if their causes are quite different. (There are those who think they can predict the stock market by the outcome of the Super Bowl.) The environmental movement is rooted in observable natural phenomena, while the women's movement in its current phase owes more to the civil rights movement. Many, many people of both sexes have been drawn to ecological activism with a devotion easily comparable to that of ecofeminists.

The ecofeminists' wholesale denigration of men is likewise quite indefensible, morally and factually. It is not even remotely compatible with Christianity, nor can the specific charges against men be squared with common-sense observation. Most men are not at heart ascetics who seek to deny the world, nor rapists, nor predatory conquerors, nor most of the (often contradictory) things they are accused of being by ecofeminist ideology, but married, with children, devoted to their families, working in cooperation with others to maintain and enhance life against the vagaries and even cruelties which the natural world can inflict. Conflict, war, and painful inequalities certainly exist, and need to be addressed and overcome; but to portray these as uniformly representing the triumph of men over women, much less the triumph of white Western men over all other human beings, is historical foolishness, representative of a desire of privileged women who make these assertions to be themselves numbered among the victims and so to recover moral legitimacy. Indeed, ecofeminism has been accused of simple scapegoating, of denying the complicity of women in ecological damage, and of forgetting that women in power can behave just as badly as men.[80]

The movement's understanding of nature is also troubled and contradictory. To assert that there is no hierarchy in nature, that all is there harmonious, is to fly in the face of brute facts like food chains. To call nature wholly nurturing, benign, and peaceful, in order to celebrate the feminine as the truly "natural," is willfully to ignore disease, volcanoes, and drought, which are equally part of nature. To assert that "We need to remake the earth in a way that converts our minds to nature's logic of ecological harmony"[81] is to gloss over the way that "harmony" is achieved: the big fish eat the little ones.

An alternative to this romantic denial of the obvious, taken by other writers, is simply to accept the violence and bloodshed of the natural world as part of a greater good, the good of the planetary whole. But inevitably that reasoning leads to accepting with equanimity the evolutionary or catastrophic demise of the human race. The world may well be better off without us. And that line of thought brings ecofeminism to the same anti-humanistic conclusion embedded in biocentrism.

The movement's specific theology is also morally and historically objectionable. Explicit rejection of Western monotheism is the course of choice among ecofeminists, who accept in its place a frank paganism, perhaps overlooking the sometimes bloody rites that are part of archaic religions. At least these women are being consistent with the principles of their movement. The task is harder for those (fewer in number, one judges) who wish to retain the Western tradition. By their own admission, they set out to revise the Judeo-Christian heritage according to a goal they wish to achieve. Selections are made from the deposit of faith according to the cause to be served. Of course this way of interpretation is an old, old trick, but it has not gained credibility by its antiquity. Maintaining authenticity means keeping to a fundamental honesty in presenting the religion, honoring its historic integrity.

Lovelock's Gaian hypothesis is subjected to a similarly procrustean treatment. His thesis does imply a certain teleology: the earth behaves purposively, to maintain a habitable environment. But as this conclusion cannot be established by the science he uses, he can only suggest it, and rather modestly not specifically claim it, quite unlike his admirers in the "new Age" and ecofeminist circles who like to think he has shown that the earth itself is worthy of worship. That is neither his claim nor his intention.

In the end of the day it seems better to refuse the willful theological alterations and accept the Western monotheistic tradition for the very reason that ecofeminists by and large reject it, that it permits, encourages, even requires as a duty of responsible stewardship of God-given creation, that we exercise our common sense in the service of rational anthropocentrism.

Environmental Politics

A proper environmental ethic, one that is steeped in a religiously-grounded concern for the protection and enhancement of human life in a healthy biosphere, must, of course, eventuate in responsible public policy. What shall we really *do* to translate our ethical imperatives, our vision, into action? What does stewardship of the earth actually require?

Unfortunately, in order to proceed we will have to make judgments on competing sets of facts offered to us by the natural sciences. "Experts" of apparently comparable competence, equally credentialed by their Ph.D.s and their prestigious appointments, speak contradictory wisdom to our untutored lay ears. In this situation plotting appropriate courses of action is extraordinarily difficult. Worse yet, from the viewpoint of this book, this is an area—validity of scientific claim—where a specifically Christian judgment is mostly unavailable. Let us conduct a *tour d'horizon* to see how this is so.

I

Those who insist that the evidence for a real crisis is all about us have a difficult legacy of false alarms to overcome. For thirty years and more they and their predecessors have been predicting things that did not happen: worldwide famine in the 1970s, a permanent oil shortage, escalating mineral prices as shortages loomed, even (before global warming became the scare of choice) the perceptible dawn of a new ice age. None of these happened, and the insistence of their forecasters that disaster has only been postponed has consequently lost some credibility. One is reminded of those prophets who have confidently predicted and set—and reset—the date for the end of the world and the Second Coming, only to see their disillusioned followers drift away. (We will likely hear from more of them as the second millennium approaches.) To cite the classic literary references, it's the Chicken Little or "cry wolf" effect. Still, before we fall into a possibly dangerous complacency about the environment, it would be well to look more closely at the competing claims.[82]

Global Warming and the Greenhouse Effect

The thesis here is by now familiar to us all: recent increases in the temperature of the earth—a 0.5 degree Celsius increase since 1860—signal the start of a dangerous climatic shift brought on by human activity, principally the burning of fossil fuels. Atmospheric levels of carbon dioxide have increased 13 percent since 1950, and that, along with other trace gasses like methane, chlorofluorocarbons, and nitrous oxides, have created a kind of reflecting shell that traps the sun's heat. An increase of 1.5 degree Celsius over pre-industrial levels could cause climate alterations falling outside the range of any experienced in the last ten thousand years. We are feeling the effects already in summer heat waves and drought. The rise by the mid twenty-first century could be anywhere from 3 to 9 degrees, an increase comparable to that which ended the last ice age. The results might include a rise in the ocean level with attendant coastal flooding, more severe storms, extinctions of plants and animals that could not adapt quickly enough, health hazards as disease-carrying insects expand their range, and vast changes in agricultural regions.

Furthermore, we have to act now to slow this process, which in any case will continue at some level, since the gasses are already in the atmosphere. Those who insist on this scenario had their way at the 1992 "earth summit" in Rio, where the United Nations Framework Convention on Global Climate Change was adopted, its stated purpose being to stabilize greenhouse gasses and prevent dangerous human interference with climate patterns.

Those arguing against the theory say ocean temperatures are virtually unchanged in the last century, and land warming should have been much more if the alarmists are right. The increase is well within the normal climatic variation and need not be attributed to human activity. In fact, confounding those who like to tell us that too many of the hottest years on record have been in the past decade and a half, earth's atmospheric temperature has remained unchanged or even actually *cooled* slightly in that time, according to satellite measurements. The heat-trapping gasses have indeed increased sharply, but without noticeable effect on the earth's temperature. Ironically, the clouds caused by some pollutants, e.g. burning coal, as well as clouds caused by the change wrought by carbon dioxide in vapor convection currents, may contribute to a *cooling* effect. Also, increased carbon dioxide may actually increase vegetation growth and be overall beneficial. This was the case in earlier geological ages when earth was covered with lush vegetation. Deserts could bloom, the soil would be improved, and ground water would be purer.

The alarmists' computer models do not in fact account for what has happened in this century and are thus not to be trusted. If they cannot account for the past, we can hardly believe them about the future. Computer models are not empirical data in any case, and are scientifically suspect for that reason. One should beware of extrapolating from climate trends that aren't long enough. We have data for scarcely one century, a small blip in the earth's history; and climate shifts can be very long term indeed. It would help our sense of perspective to recall that speculation of twenty years ago mentioned above, that "recent trends" indicated we could be in for another ice age, or at least a "little ice age" like that of the sixteenth to eighteenth centuries. If we can extend our perspective back to the last ice age, ten thousand years ago, we might note that the primitive humanity of that time adapted beautifully to *their* global warming. How much more readily can modern technological humanity adapt? It is simply not true that human life is always ill-served by climate change.

Finally, the steps necessary to halt the greenhouse effect would be severe and costly and wasteful, e.g. trying to double the fuel efficiency of cars (bucking the law of diminishing returns), or investing in unneeded synthetic fuels. They would have a negligible effect on climate change in any case.

The Ozone Hole

Here again we have conflicting appraisals. According to one side in the debate, endorsed by the 1995 Nobel chemistry prize, we are losing the protective layer of atmospheric ozone which filters out harmful ultraviolet rays that cause skin cancer. Besides the celebrated hole over the Antarctic, the amount of ozone over the temperate zone of the Northern Hemisphere is also apparently thinning. As a result of these warnings an "ultraviolet index" has been added to many local weather reports—an indication that the ozone alarm has taken hold of the popular mind. The Montreal Protocol of 1987, and its 1990 sequel in London, are a result of the scare. These agreements to end the production or use of chlorofluorocarbons (CFCs) by 1996, particularly as refrigerants, will be very costly.

The other side agrees that there is evidence for some ozone loss (though not over the Northern Hemisphere; they see that as a pure false alarm), but doubts that CFCs are at fault, noting that the amount of ozone varies naturally. Moreover the ill effects of the ozone loss have not been proven, and in fact there has been very little increase in the amount of ultraviolet radiation reaching the ground—a harmless amount at that. But if indeed the ozone hole is caused, or exacerbated, by the release of certain chemicals, even if the warnings are right, the current and growing abatement of these releases should enable the hole eventually to shrink. Indeed, the process has already proceeded faster than predicted and there is no further need to ban CFCs in such vital uses as refrigeration.

Perhaps this is the place to note that James Lovelock's Gaia hypothesis, that the earth is "alive" in the sense that all parts work together in a self-adjusting whole to create homeostasis, means that the biosphere is so resilient and adaptable that it can overcome such chemical insults. Lovelock does not worry about ozone depletion or pollution, to the distress, no doubt, of his ecological admirers. The admiration, in fact, seems to be one way: He admits he is not a friend of "most environmentalists," whom he characterizes as "misanthropes" and "Luddites"[83]—a not inappropriate charge, as we shall see.

Pollution

Chemicals used in agriculture and industry, whether intentionally added to food and other products, or released as waste, accidentally or on purpose, stand accused of poisoning the environment to the detriment of the health of all living things, humans included. Exposure to them, it is claimed, has especially increased the incidence of cancer. Environmental activists have discovered and dramatized these hazards and led public campaigns for controls, or clean-ups, or outright bans. They have been highly successful, too, as witness our clean air and water laws and special funds to clean up toxic dumps. Surely skeptics cannot find fault with this important public service.

The service is real and valued, acknowledge the critics, and in some cases right on target, as in the damage to wildlife from DDT and other pesticides. But the alleged crises are also frequently overstated, in particular instances wrong, and wrongly addressed. Actual exposure to toxic chemicals in the United States causes an almost undetectable, and vanishing, number of cases of cancer or chronic illness, not to be compared in effect to the naturally occurring carcinogens in our diet. Many specific alarms about contamination with toxic materials have proven to be overinflated or simply wrong—the Alar and dioxin cases are good examples. The activists' use of experimental evidence is often deeply flawed, as when large doses kill laboratory animals and the test is extrapolated to predict danger to humans from even small doses. The alarmists have defied scientific knowledge that it is the level of dosage that causes harm, and instead insisted, without any valid evidence, that the only safe level of exposure to toxic chemicals is zero. Thus their "going to zero" program, effectively an outright ban, is a scientifically inappropriate response, except in the case of a very few persistent and cumulative pesticides that endanger wildlife. In fact, conclude the skeptics, while it is right and useful to keep a close watch on the use of toxic chemicals, there seems to be no credible evidence so far that their increasing use in modern American life has raised the death rate at all.

Much the same can be said of other dramatized cases of pollution, that they have been exaggerated and exploited far beyond their real effects. Exxon is probably right that Prince William Sound had mostly recovered from the *Exxon Valdez* oil spill within two years, partly from clean-up efforts and partly from natural processes (and that the damage awards were excessive). Pollution from auto emissions is better (lead levels in air have dropped 95 percent since unleaded fuels were introduced twenty years ago) and will continue to improve as old cars are phased out. Smog has been reduced. Many waterways are cleaner, fit for fishing and even drinking, and so on. As the wealth of a nation grows, instead of polluting more, it spends more money on pollution control and becomes cleaner.

This is not an argument against environmental regulation, however, for environmental laws have been to a large extent responsible for these improvements; and in any case, progress has been uneven, or in some cases, like the decline of freshwater ecosystems, actually absent altogether. We still have a long way to go. But the environmental watchdogs need to be much more careful with their language of panic and crisis, and with their science, lest they lose their credibility.

Note, not entirely by the way, that in poorer countries the major causes of pollution of air and water—and the resultant millions of deaths—are not the exotic products of modern industrial life, but smoke from burning wood and cow dung and the failure to separate sewage from drinking water. Central energy production by hydroelectric dams or generating plants burning fossil fuels, and large-scale water supply and sewage projects, would be environmental *progress* for these peoples, anathema though that might be to many Western environmentalists. Such power would also make refrigeration possible (which solar power does not), resulting in a major health improvement. A good case can even be made for allowing the use of DDT in malaria-stricken areas like tropical Africa, on the grounds that human welfare ought to take precedence over harm to wildlife.

Loss of Fertile Land and Forests

I am more worried about this issue, but that may be one of those personal biases that must be allowed. I am, as I said, a sometime countryman, and I love the land. I tend to think organic farming is a very good idea, and I wince when any part of the rich soil of the river valley where I live is paved over. In any case, the argument of the alarmists, who alarm me, is roughly as follows.

Since 1950 the world has lost one-fifth of its topsoil from cropland and one-fifth of its tropical rain forests. Forest area the size of Finland is lost every year, and most of the rain forests will be gone in fifty years at the current rate of cutting. The uses of the rain forests are many: they are the source of half the world's flora and fauna, of plants possibly used for medicines not yet discovered, and potential new crops. The trees are critical for consuming carbon dioxide and producing oxygen, so their loss would have great and unpredictable effects on climate. Lovelock excepts the rain forests from his general thesis that a resilient earth can recover and adapt, considering them, and wetlands as well, indispensable to planetary health.

There seems to be little doubt that rapacious economic interests are a large part of the cause of the damage, and that the interests of native peoples have been flagrantly disregarded in the process. The push of small farmers into virgin lands, with slash-and-burn techniques, has hurt, too, an expansion driven by population pressure along with a desire to escape poverty. But there are too many farmers to practice this traditional method, which allows the land to regenerate only if left fallow for a number of years; and one can see the inevitable sad result in places like Haiti and Rwanda. The forests are gone, the soils degraded, the land eroded. In marginal dry lands the deserts expand where once people were able to farm or graze animals, and the term "desertification" has been added to the vocabulary of ecological crisis. Harvests are no longer getting bigger, and food prices will shortly begin to rise everywhere as scarcity sets in.

Environmentalists answer the expected charge that their land conservation policies would lead to starvation among poor people in the third world by suggesting some economic advantages to their ideas. First-world tourists would come to admire these virgin lands, bringing their money; "ecotourism" will counter poverty. Fees could be charged to first-world corporations for genetically valuable stocks discovered and taken from these natural areas for new medicines and crops, instead of allowing these powerful commercial interests to keep all the profits from their use of someone else's biological resources. The preservation of wild land will actually help, not harm, local populations, since these are indigenous peoples who have always made a living from their forests and do not want it developed anyway. All too often they are at odds with their own governments, and the international environmental agencies are pleased to be thought their saviors. Fortunately those governments can sometimes be induced to save their virgin lands, instead of developing them, by so-called debt-for-nature swaps, by which part of their international debt, owed to foreign banks and governments, is forgiven in exchange for preserving large tracts. The saved lands need not be pure wilderness set-asides, either, but can be used for water conservation projects or the continued sale of their renewable products. Thus preservation can be seen as an economic asset, not a sacrifice.

We should note, too, that this is not by any means only a third world problem. The United States government builds roads into public forests at taxpayer expense, thus facilitating logging which would be much less profitable, if at all, if the roads were not subsidized. American policies have encouraged over-grazing of semi-arid Western lands, subsidizing this practice by cheap usage fees, below what would be market rates; and this policy is highly resistant to change, since it has created interests dependent on it. (Save the family ranch!) It is furthermore ecologically unsound to encourage meat-eating, as domestic livestock are an inefficient way to convert the sun's energy into food, and the animals create methane that exacerbates the greenhouse effect. (The cattlemen, of course, argue otherwise, that cattle turn lands not good for crop raising into useful sources of food.)

Thus, in round summary form, runs the indictment against current world land-use practices. There is, however, another side to this apparently dolorous picture.

There are ways to make a forest productive of useful timber without disastrous clear cutting, and ways to feed growing populations without degrading the soils. It appears possible, with new varieties of fast-growing trees, to achieve forest restoration and at the same time support an inevitably expanding rural population on the land. Selective logging, preserving the trees that produce marketable fruits, latex, and other products, would make a tropical forest an economic resource indefinitely. Some countries have recognized that they are expending their timber capital faster than it can be regrown, and have imposed bans on the export of raw logs, e.g. Thailand, Indonesia, the Philippines, and Malaysia (but only on the mainland part of the country). This is a hopeful sign, even if one must admit that often the bans are partial, or unenforced, and that the cut logs continue to be shipped in quantity to the United States and elsewhere, above all to Japan. In any case, with better woodland management and technological improvements in utilization of the trees, the world's wood requirements could be met on a small fraction of the planet's forested land, leaving the rest to shelter biodiversity and cleanse the air of carbon dioxide.

Better farming methods are also gaining favor, methods that take advantage of natural processes rather than practices that have contaminating effects on ground water or lead to toxic runoff. These methods are varied and specific to the region and crop, and are determined largely by good scientific study, e.g., crop rotation to fix nitrogen, tillage methods which reduce erosion, biological pest control instead of insecticides, organic fertilizing if a local livestock industry is practicable, and genetic improvement of crops. Genetically engineered plants are just a logical extension of plant breeding and can reduce, though not eliminate, the need for synthetic fertilizers, fungicides, and insecticides. Continuing refinements of these latter products themselves, through science, will further reduce the need for their use.

Anyway the crisis is not yet upon us. The prophets of imminent famine have been proven wrong, for food is more abundant and cheaper, worldwide, than ever before. It is actually possible, perhaps for the first time in human history, to put an end to hunger. Soil erosion has been exaggerated, and the amount of production lost to erosion can and is easily made up by advances in agricultural science. Moreover soil quality loss is not permanent, but can be restored by organic farming (from the plant roots themselves, mainly), over time and at some cost, to be sure; but the problem is economic, not environmental. Eventually the current processes of production will change, as processes always have.

As for "desertification," that is another false alarm. In 1972 the United States Agency for International Development said the Sahara Desert was moving southward at the rate of thirty miles a year. But data from the decade of the 1980s show the Sahara receding with increased rainfall, not steadily expanding. There is no discernible overall trend. Of course long-term data don't exist, so we don't really know what is happening over an extended time. But other records indicate that climate is the major factor in the movement of desert back and forth, with human activity a contributing but much less important factor. When a drought period ends, the dry land ecosystem bounces back. Indicated policy might not be much more complicated than old-fashioned erosion control. In any case, the term "desertification" has fallen out of favor with the scientific community, though it is politically useful to dry land countries seeking international aid. The African countries saved the term at the Rio Conference by expanding its definition to include the degradation of arid lands from various causes; for purposes of international politics, it no longer means refers only to the encroachment of deserts.

There are many issues of justice involved in land-use decisions, and I will return to some of them below in discussing third world development. But the one issue which trumps the others is surely the prevention of world hunger. To feed a growing world population (which will grow whether we like it or not), we will obviously have to grow more food; and the only realistic hope beyond altered farming methods, and needed as a supplement to them, is biotechnology and smart chemistry, not a Luddite reaction which would cause starvation. But this necessity need not alarm anyone but the most committed technology hater; for in fact, high-yield modern farming actually saves land, since lower yields would mean more land under cultivation, and hence not in wild pasture or forest.

Loss of Species

The environmentalist argument, put energetically by writers like E. O. Wilson and Norman Meyers, is that because of human activity we are losing the great variety of plant and animal species which has characterized our geological age, and that the loss is accelerating dangerously and to our harm. Maybe one-fifth of all species will disappear in the next twenty years. One of the most visible examples is that global fish stocks are being depleted; once productive regions like Georges Bank have been closed to allow recovery, and many varieties seem to have disappeared altogether. Other examples are legion. Loss of diversity will leave us without many sources of new drugs or new disease-resistant crops or other food sources, and in general will reduce the earth's resiliency and adaptability. The earth might eventually recover its diversity, with a new mix of course, but only after millions of years; and by then it will be too late for humanity, which will have joined the extinct species.

Granted, reply the skeptics, we are in an age where species numbers are declining. But such losses and greater ones have happened before, and new varieties always emerge. Sixty-five million years ago a mass extinction wiped out two-thirds of all species, but the earth recovered its fecundity. Lynn Margulis, James Lovelock's co-worker and a famed biologist herself, says that "99.99% of the species which have existed since the 'Cambrian explosion' 540 million years ago are now extinct."[84] Extinctions are part of natural evolution, and the current loss may not even be exceptional.

Measures to protect particular species from extinction, such as the well-known Endangered Species Act, which lists some 950 threatened varieties in the United States, are of doubtful value. Whether it has actually rescued any species is a matter of argument. Internationally the high-profile effort to "save the whales" illustrates the ambiguity of these projects. The International Whaling Commission (IWC) instituted a moratorium on whaling, achieved with great difficulty and in the face of widespread cheating by Japan and the (then) Soviet Union, but then declined to lift it when one species, the minke, once again became, or was determined to be, plentiful. As a result Norway and Iceland resigned from the IWC, complaining with some justice that the ban, instituted to save species, was being continued under an animal welfare ideology to which they had not agreed. The conservationist purpose of the ban sank in the confusion. Likewise the famous "seal wars" of the 1970s, against the sealers who took the white pups of harp seals, were animal welfare campaigns carried out with a rather minimal regard for truth and none at all for environmental concerns, since the seals are plentiful.

Consumption of Resources

The alarmist view can be put bluntly and simply. The basic resources we need are finite—minerals from the earth, arable soil, fresh water, sheer space for the natural world to live and produce the substances on which life depends. As the human population grows, we use these up. Technology will not save us, because increased technology leads to ever greater consumption of these environmental resources. Even renewable resources cannot keep up with human economic growth. We cannot escape the limits imposed by the natural ecosystem, and on our current course we will "overshoot the carrying capacity of the earth" and crash. We must therefore curb our economic and population growth sharply and soon.

This is the scenario that was given dramatic expression in the Club of Rome's 1972 report *The Limits to Growth*, in which another of those famous pseudo-scientific computer models predicted the exhaustion of a long list of resources, at least within this century, unless economic and population growth were halted almost immediately. But they were dead wrong. Not only are the minerals on their "imminent exhaustion" list still plentiful, but most are actually cheaper than in 1972. In the best-known case, they predicted the exhaustion of oil at the end of two decades, but when the time came there was instead a worldwide glut of oil with resultant downward pressure on prices. The supply of crude oil has actually increased over the past forty years. Again, the U.S. Geological Survey in 1974 predicted a ten-year supply of natural gas at that year's production methods and price, but not long afterward the American Gas Association claimed there was enough gas to last from one hundred to twenty-five hundred years at present levels of consumption. I participated in an international conference in 1974, under the spell of the doomsayers, in which one scientist said off-handedly that one could work out "on the back of an envelope" the amount of oil left in the ground, while another said with equal assurance that "no one has any idea how much is down there."

Lay people are entitled to ask for an explanation of this confusion among their scientists, and a likely candidate lies in the failure of many scientific specialists to understand the economics of supply and demand. Demand for a resource raises its price, and the price increase eventually stabilizes the demand. A high price spurs the development of alternatives (including conservation), which in turn lowers the price of the original resource. The oil price increase inflicted by the Organization of Petroleum Exporting Countries' cartel in defiance of the normal laws of supply and demand led to conservation measures and increased production outside the OPEC countries. OPEC then had trouble keeping the price up. In fact, thanks to these natural laws of economic behavior and the technological ingenuity which they encourage, the price of gasoline in the United States, adjusted for inflation, has not risen in years.

Scarcity, in other words, is not just a measure of physical bulk, of quantity, but also of cost, which affects availability. This is the point which is missed by those who think of finiteness only in terms of physical measures, and explains why an economist, Julian Simon, actually won a 1980 bet (by one account not very graciously paid) from Paul Ehrlich, one of the more famous scientific gloom-mongers, that raw material prices would decline over a ten-year period rather than increase, as the scarcity alarmists like Ehrlich had predicted. Of course scientifically-trained environmentalists reply for their part that economists don't understand absolute physical limitations. But in any case it is a fact that the prices of most raw materials have been decreasing not just for ten years but over the whole of human history, even as population and demand grow. The trend is likely to continue, say the optimists. Electric power will be cheaper; solar technology, aided by developments in superconductivity, will be much improved; fuel efficiency will continue to increase, and we may even see the end of the age of fossil fuels; and new resources, developed in response to scarcities elsewhere and to economic opportunities, will come on line.

Population Growth

Throughout this brief review of ecological flash points the subject of population growth has kept cropping up. Is this, perhaps, the master problem, the most important element in our environmental "crisis"? Certainly the dramatic growth of human numbers is a fact. Four-fifths of the people alive today have been born since World War II. The world's population in 1900 was 1.6 billion; it is now 5.7 billion, mostly because of a rapid decline in death rates. Every day we add 250,000 more to the total. It is exponential growth, and hence deserves the term "explosion." Even if birth rates fall we will reach 8–10 billion in another century or less, and maybe 14 billion if the rates do not decrease.

This is certain eventually to lead to a reduction in food-per-person, the Malthusian prediction; it is already happening in Africa, despite new ways of raising food. It would seem to be a matter of common sense that a world population that will double in the next fifty years (at the current rate) will put a terrible and unmanageable strain on the environment. Resources, including water, timber, and fertile soil, will be exhausted. Global warming will get worse. The earth will not be able to absorb our wastes. Famine and disease haunt our future. Nature will kill us by the millions if we don't take rapid and severe measures ourselves, one way or another lowering birth rates below death rates.

How shall we accomplish this goal? Global contraceptive campaigns are the most humane way. The demand is there; and in countries where it has been met, especially in East Asia, the birth rate has dropped dramatically. Rising standards of living, especially the education of women, also reduce births considerably. But if humane methods don't work, something else must be used, lest nature's altogether amoral processes, starvation and disease, do the job for us.

That, in a nutshell, is the argument of the environmental population controllers; and they have perhaps persuaded most of the world that they are right. Birth control campaigns have taken hold in populous countries all over the globe; and that message dominated the United Nations' "International Conference on Population and Development" in Cairo, which adopted a program aiming to hold the world's population level to 7.27 billion by 2015.

But is the situation really that dire? The predictions so far seem off target. Paul Ehrlich warned in *The Population Bomb* (1968) that the "bomb" would go off in the 1970s: "The battle to feed all of humanity is over. In the 1970s . . . hundreds of millions of people are going to starve to death."[85] He was quite wrong. He said it was "fantasy" to think that India could ever feed itself, but that country now exports food. I remember telling a startled colleague at the time the book was published that it was "the worst serious book I've ever read." I will admit now to a little overstatement (but not much), because the book was intended to popularize and dramatize the issue for effect, and it was very successful at that. But still, one must ask of this book, and others like it, where they went wrong. They certainly underestimated the ability of the human race to reduce its fecundity. The fertility rate of the developing countries, supposedly the place where the problem is most serious, has dropped from 6.0 children per woman in 1970 to 3.7 now. Since 2.2 children per woman is the point of zero population growth, the rate is already more than halfway to zero. By some estimates the decline in fertility presages a net world population *decrease* during the second part of the twenty-first century!

Nor is population pressure the cause of famine or poverty. Famines have other causes, like droughts, rats, food spoilage from lack of refrigeration, inadequate transportation, civil war, and inept government. Poverty, likewise, has many causes, and population pressure need not be one of them, as we can see by some quick comparisons. Some prosperous countries, like the United States or Canada or Australia, have few people per square mile, while others, like the Netherlands and Japan, have managed to combine density with wealth. (But the environmentalist will say at once that these two countries do not live on their own resources, but depend on imports, and that therefore their experience cannot be universalized.) Some of the very poor countries are thinly populated, and some of them are indeed thick with human habitation. It appears that density is not in itself the critical factor in prosperity. (Even with a world population of ten billion, human settlements would occupy only 2 percent of the earth's land.) Prosperity depends not on the right number of people, but on a social system that allows them to produce wealth. This is not to say, however, that social and economic problems would not be easier to address in many countries (for example, Egypt) if their population level would stabilize, nor that population pressure is not a problem in selected localities. The point is that it is not a *global* problem. And that, in another nutshell, is the case against the population controllers.

We could proceed thus through a number of other topics, e.g. *acid rain*. Produced by coal-fired industries and once thought to be killing forests and lakes downwind, it was found on careful examination to be doing nothing of the sort. How about *nuclear energy*? It is a more complicated issue, of course, but we come to the same result. On the one side are the "Pandora's Box" and "Faustian bargain" critics who say that radiation from the use of nuclear power will cause cancer and genetic mutations, that the accident at Chernobyl was a convincing demonstration of the inherent dangers, that nuclear wastes cannot be safely stored for the thousands of years they will be radioactive. On the other side are those who tell us that the environmental and health hazards even now are far less than those from mining and burning coal, that the technology is likely to be much safer in the future, that the natural background radiation reaching us from the ground and from space is hundreds of times greater than any we get from human production, that a single coast-to-coast airplane ride exposes us to five times the radiation we would get from living right next door to a nuclear power plant for a whole year, and that the very small amount of nuclear waste not reprocessed or naturally and quickly losing its radioactivity can be bonded to glass, encased in steel, and safely stored indefinitely in stable underground facilities.

And so we could go on through waste disposal, plastics, electromagnetic fields, and more. But by now the lesson is abundantly clear. We are confronted with diametrically opposing claims and asked to make choices most of us are ill-equipped to make. There is, moreover, very little of specifically or uniquely Christian content to such decisions. Nevertheless a theologically informed understanding of human nature will help us a good deal to sort them out. We should, of course, be held to standards of honesty and clarity and cool-headed reason; and we should require of all partisans that their advocacy not come at the cost of truthfulness. We should beware of choosing based entirely on our trust—or distrust—of the messenger, though to some extent we must inevitably take such judgments into account. Many environmental optimists, for example, are business people or "business friendly," and hence are suspect to those who, for other reasons, distrust the business world. Many who are skeptical of the environmental warnings are likely to be associated in the public mind with one political party or political orientation, and the environmentalists with the opposite end of the political spectrum. But these classifications do only rough justice to the picture, and in any case such prior dispositions should not by themselves determine our factual conclusions. It is not necessarily "conservative" to be skeptical of environmental alarms, nor is it necessarily "liberal" to be an environmentalist. These political labels ought to have no bearing on our judgments about scientific fact.

It also behooves us to be appropriately suspicious of the self-interest of rival claimants, not only producers and users of possibly harmful or wasteful substances who want to protect their economic interests, and scientists and agencies whose environmental programs depend on government funding (and who campaign for funds by press release of speculative and frightening data), but also the environmental organizations themselves, whose budgets, power, and very existence depend on giving the impression that they are saving the public and the planet. This, too, like critical awareness of our trust level, is a healthy caveat, though self-interest does not automatically disqualify a claim.

Because we are asked to make factual judgments, we will also have to realize that we are not choosing whole sides, as if we were voting a straight party ticket, but appraising each issue on its separate merits. We might, for example, judge the global warming scare to be overblown, but think there is some substance to the concern about ozone depletion.

It is also important to factor in the influences of desire and fear on our judgment. If we have a tendency to choose what we want to be the case, we may favor the judgments of the optimists and forget to apply to environmental history that legislated caution of the mutual fund prospectus, "past performance is no guarantee of future results." There is an ecological version of the uncertainty principle, and we ought to leave a margin for error, lest the dire predictions finally do come true. If, on the other hand, we tend toward a natural pessimism, we are likely to be swayed by each new environmental alarm we hear and to adopt worst-case scenarios. Both tendencies corrupt our judgment, however subtly.

We need also to be aware of the costs of environmental programs, the better to embed them in our larger choices about the use of our social resources. To put it simply, do they cost more than they are worth? There is nothing wrong with cost-benefit analysis, often thought by environmentalists to be a stalling device to avoid action. In fact, however, we all make choices, based on comparative costs, as to what to do with limited resources, and it is good stewardship of those resources to do so. Some environmental laws—the "Super Fund" to clean up toxic sites appears to be a case in point—can be extraordinarily wasteful of money that could be better spent for greater public benefit. Others—clean water legislation, for example— may be judged well worth the cost.

In all these matters our duty, our responsibility, is to examine evidence as dispassionately as possible, allowing for our own biases. We must listen carefully to all voices, perhaps especially to the ones we don't want to hear. We must use our critical reason to the best of our ability, remembering that ignorance is a more important cause of environmental damage than ill will or greed.

II

The warring experts are battling for the public ear and have policies in mind. Sometimes these policies spring directly from their scientific conclusions, but often they go well beyond the science to enter realms of value choices which are quite accessible to the scrutiny of non-scientists also. So without settling the scientific disagreements here, we can and should look at the possible policy alternatives to see what these might suggest to Christian ethics.

Apocalyptic environmentalism tends to breed correspondingly radical prescriptions for social change. The very foundations of our social order must be altered, they say. We must adopt wholly new ways of living. We must think differently. This is utopian language, or, as Ronald Bailey says, millenialist.[86] Paul Ehrlich, for example, says the environmental crisis can only be overcome by a "new civilization" which will cure the "inequitable distribution of wealth and resources, racism, sexism, religious prejudice, and xenophobia."[87] Audacious programs and sweeping vision are in order. And of course we have no time left and had better change our ways at once, starting at the top. We cannot wait for the slow process of public education, though we must pursue that, too. But we had better move right now through our agencies of government to impose the necessary regulations to stave off disaster.

Since environmental problems are usually the kind that do not respect national boundaries, it is clear, says this school of thought, that world regulation is necessary. We must have global treaties—and we do, and the number is growing. At last count there were close to two hundred treaties dealing with environmental issues. On top of the heap is the proposed U.N. Sustainable Development Commission to oversee the projects agreed upon at Rio, including the preservation of biodiversity, restraining global warming, population limitation programs, and the like.

Some people have seen in this development the beginnings of the ultimate centrally planned society: extensive regulations imposed worldwide. The forerunners of this dawning world order are the population controllers—Hardin and Ehrlich and Kingsley Davis and their ideological descendants and followers[88]—who go so far as to attack the idea of human rights, because such anti-government individualism inhibits the imposition of the necessary limitations. So the totalitarian state, "in a good cause" of course, or at best a benevolent dictatorship, is on its way, its delights prefigured for us by the population policies of modern China. Is it, as Hardin smoothly says, "mutual coercion, mutually agreed upon"—or is it tyranny?[89]

Even if they are not crypto-totalitarians, many of the proponents of maintaining a steady-state in resource use are at least "planners" when it comes to political programs. They argue for rigid allocations made possible by centralized political authority able to overcome supposedly ignorant and selfish consumer desires, and this for the ultimate good of those whom they control, of course.

In short, in the perennial tug between freedom and order, much environmental thought has opted for order, suspecting freedom of being selfish and eventually greedy, hence environmentally heedless and short-sighted. Thus the common jibe that the former "reds" have become "greens," that the mentality of the former, where we pass by totalitarianism (or at least socialism) to utopia, has become the ideal of the latter. There is a common impression, which as noted above does not really have to be true, that environmentalists tend to cluster on the political Left, their optimistic detractors on the Right. Thus, archetypically, we have Barry Commoner, famous ecologist and failed politician, running for president more or less independently on a socialist and "green" platform.

This impression of convergence between socialism and environmentalism is fed by a noticeable animus in environmental thought toward capitalism, a simple feeling that that system promotes a high level of production and consumption, and that this is the cause of environmental degradation. The price mechanism in a free market economy assumes economic individualism, where things are used according to the value placed on them by those who consume them, following their own private wants. In such a system a public good like a "sustainable" society, acting for the benefit of future generations, gets short shrift if it is considered at all.

Murray Bookchin, the founder of the "social ecology" movement, is prominent among those who believe that capitalism is the major and direct cause of the environmental "crisis." Capitalism is rapacious, greedy, and so on, stressing profits above the social good—all the common complaints we have heard about it for a century, now reminted in the cause of environmentalism. "Nearly all our present ecological problems arise from deep-seated social problems," particularly "the hierarchical mentality and class relationships that so thoroughly permeate society." The fault lies in the competitive market economy, whose harsh discipline precludes attempts to be ecologically sound. "Modern capitalism is *structurally* amoral and hence impervious to any moral appeals." Its devastating ecological impact is built into the system.[90]

Bookchin's is a fairly typical reaction from the political Left. For some on this wing the ecological complaint against the market economy is perhaps a new realization, but for others it is likely that their real cause is the end of capitalism. Disappointed by the failure of Marxism, they have found in environmentalism a new cudgel for the job—although the ecological wastelands of eastern Europe must remind all of them that Marxist societies have poor environmental records.

A similar outlook prevails in the ecofeminist subdivision of environmental activism. Most ecofeminists seem convinced that capitalism is a bad system, the natural outcome in economics of the despised patriarchal drive for dominance, "a new hierarchicalism that makes women, workers, peasants, and conquered races the image of dominated nature in contrast to the Euro-American male, the true bearer of transcendent consciousness." In a capitalist economy, "nature is raped for profits." The capitalist industrial system uses "the toil of laboring bodies . . . through which the earth is despoiled and left desolate. Through the raped bodies the earth is raped."[91] Hence the predilection in this movement for some form of society theoretically not based on class or gender dominance, though enthusiasm for traditional socialism has been tempered by its authoritarianism and that poor environmental record of actual socialist societies.

Although social ecology is considerably less romantic than ecofeminism, and unlike ecofeminism preserves a real distinction between humans and nature, both share an ideal of a society formed on the model of nature, which is held to achieve harmony by consensus and cooperation. The trick is to eschew the mentality of domination. Bookchin joins the ecofeminists in believing that a "natural" society is egalitarian, not hierarchical, that it reflects "feminine values associated with care and nurture," to our sorrow later "overshadowed by masculine values associated with combative and aggressive behavior."[92]

"In nature," says ecofeminist Judith Plant, "no one species dominates. . . . [It is] organic organization." As in nature, so with women: "Consensus is a feminine form of decision-making; it is unifying, it is sharing, it is caring, it is non-dominant, it is empowering." The operative ideals are "democratic," "communal," "egalitarian," "cooperative," "non-sexist," "non-racist," "non-violent," "anti-imperialist." Political ethics in this thinking are derived from ecology, all creatures interrelated and interdependent in a compassionate harmonious whole for the mutual benefit of all, the antithesis of the reigning "false ethic of competition."[93]

Although "green" politics is thus markedly to the "left" in terms of the usual categories, there are some forms of it which do not fit the neat parallelism with traditional socialism. Especially should we note those "greens" who are opposed to large-scale industrialism and prefer local over central controls. The society of the future, they say, will have to be anti-industrial in some way, with correspondingly dramatically altered lifestyles, and built around local economies. Devotees of this program extol the thought of E. F. Schumacher (*Small Is Beautiful*) and his program of "appropriate technology," which rejects large-scale centralized industrial organization in favor of local controls giving people more power over their own work. "Bioregionalism" is the environmentalist name for this decentralization, meaning that the organization of economic life should reflect the natural advantages of a given locality or region and explicitly not depend on free trade in an impersonal global economy.[94]

On the other side of the ledger it is somewhat easier to describe an environmentalism compatible with capitalism than to make coherent sense out of the sometimes confusing and contradictory world of "green" politics. Most people—or at least most Americans—are probably at heart "moderates," tinkerers, gradualists, who would rather address environmental problems piecemeal than initiate a social or economic revolution. Let us beware the crisis mongers, they say, and not rush off half-cocked, lest we pay steep prices for small gains (or no gains at all). We will vote for specific regulations that seem to promise results we want, like clean air and water. These laws will shift the cost of pollution to the producers, of course; but that is not only compatible with capitalism, but actually required by it: the costs of production are fully accounted for and enter into the price of the final product, as is proper.

We could actually use the market mechanisms of capitalism even better than we do, substituting financial incentives for direct regulation. Tax breaks, effluent fees, and user charges of various sorts would provide continuing incentives for the desired behavior, more efficiently and effectively than simply satisfying the minimum requirements of legislation. More land would be conserved if reduced taxes offset the lost opportunity cost of developing it. Fewer pollutants would enter the air and water if every reduction saved money in fees.[95]

Pushing this same line of thought even further is the school of "free-market environmentalism," which would privatize resources as far as practicable, the better to harness natural human self-interest in preserving them, and allow their exchange in the market, so that scarcity could be controlled by the price mechanism. The basic assumption of this school is that the market allocates resources to their highest valued use, and the price mechanism determines that value. Under the gradualist approach of tax and fee incentives outlined above, it is still the government that determines the goals and the values. Free marketers, noting the threat to liberty when central authority imposes values, argue that environmental values ought to be defined as what private individuals actually want. And, they add, we will find that sustainable use of resources is best served by owners who desire to preserve their value, because it is in their economic interest to do so. To avoid the famous "tragedy of the commons," where public property is exhausted by individuals seeking their own gain from it, get rid of the commons. Privatize everything, or virtually everything.

We are confronted here with an ancient problem that never yields easily to solution, the conflict between individual rights and the public welfare. Environmental lawsthat restrict the use of private property, e.g., limits on timber cutting to preserve endangered species, or prohibitions on draining and building on ecologically valuable wetlands, are one current focus of this perennial dispute. One side believes that owners should be compensated for this de facto "taking" of their land (if it has to occur at all), that the public owes something to private landowners who are required to be the stewards of the public good that is biodiversity. The other side holds that owners should not be paid for refraining from harming the public good, as environmentalists define that good, any more than we would pay polluters for not polluting. These disputes are never easy to resolve in a democracy, certainly not in one as individualistic as ours is.

Before we submit these conflicting views to ethical appraisal, there remains to be noted a fringe sector of radical environmentalism which has turned to violence. The degree of radicalism, and hence the prescription for cure, varies. For some the devil is modern science and technology, and the corresponding cure is a dispersed and pastoral society. A few others locate the fall from grace further back, in the primitive turn to agriculture and settled societies, which enabled the population to boom; hence their prescription for a return to the nomadic hunter-gatherer state. Others, including many ecofeminists, find monotheism to be the primal fault, hence we need to return to pagan polytheism. Still others, the most radical of all, say the trouble is at root the human presence itself, the "cancer" in nature; and they accordingly celebrate the life process which will continue after our extinction. All shades are scornful of mainstream environmentalism, as represented by the Sierra Club, the National Audubon Society, the Environmental Defense Fund, the National Wildlife Federation, and the Wilderness Society, among others, as mere reformers, "rearranging the deck chairs on the Titanic," instead of working for fundamental change.

When it comes to a political program, radical environmental thought is, for the most part, content to preach and proclaim, and, in the end of the day, work with the mainstream gradualists it despises ideologically. Yet radical thought, fueled by the crisis mentality of the alarmists and the unshakable convictions of true believers, can also produce radical action. And so it happens that the academic biocentrists, and perhaps particularly their "deep ecology" extremes (Naess, Devall, Sessions) have seen their practical coalition-building strategy and their (perhaps *pro forma*) nonviolence give way to the risky confrontationalism of Greenpeace and the open violence of Edward Abbey, Dave Foreman, and the "Earth First!" saboteurs. The sabotage, or "ecotage" or "monkey-wrenching," as they called it, included practices like destroying bulldozers or driving spikes into trees to thwart (and threaten) loggers. They praised like-minded protesters in other countries (let us call them "ecoterrorists") who have blown up offending projects, even at the cost of human life. They even muttered darkly about coming "ecowars" against countries like Brazil whose development policies they see as a threat to the global climate.

It may seem surprising that there should be such a violent fringe element at all; but in fact the commitment to the fundamental principle that nature takes precedence over any human activity which might harm it is so strong a belief, so thoroughly rooted in ideological conviction, that fanaticism in its defense seems all but inevitable. The saboteurs—in their righteousness they hate being called vandals—have invoked the classic ethical language of civil disobedience to justify their actions, but failed to honor the twin commitments of that tradition to nonviolence and to acceptance of the lawful penalties for their actions. Some have gone further and appealed to the doctrine of just war, combat in defense of the rights of the planet, assuming that the planet has rights, and that these warriors are somehow appointed to come to its defense, since it cannot speak for itself.[96]

III

What shall we make of all these competing visions? Is a Christian judgment at all possible here? While it is worth remembering that religious endorsement of political systems has had, shall we modestly and humbly say, a rather spotty historical record, we are not without ethical resources in these matters.

Christian ethics has always known that the needs of individuals and the community must both be served, that they often exist in tension, and that the proper balance is not easy to achieve. It is the individual who has God-given worth, a dignity bestowed by our

Creator, a value that cannot be taken away by any collective-minded society. Thinking in this mode, we argue for as much personal self-determination as possible, for freedom from central authority, for consensual exchanges in a free market. Forcing someone to do something is inherently bad. Defining the good by government edict is too much authoritarianism. (The old communist says to his son, "Comes the revolution, we will all eat strawberries." Protests the child, "But I don't *like* strawberries." Reply: "Comes the revolution, you *will* like strawberries.")

We invoke also the traditional Christian principle of subsidiarity, that matters should be administered at the lowest level possible. Local management is more effective than distant regulation, often (but not always!) better able to protect resources than a national government, whose land-use schemes should be tempered by the local wisdom of the people directly affected. It is surely clear, ethically speaking, that people should have a voice in decisions that affect their daily lives. One cannot love one's neighbor without knowing the neighbor's need, and one cannot know that need well without asking. Top-down authoritarianism is highly suspect from a Christian perspective, and usually inefficient from an economic perspective as well.

But there is another powerful strand in Christian social thought which must be kept in tension with the bias toward personal freedom, and that is service for the common good—by which, in accordance with the theme of this book, I mean primarily human welfare. The common good, moreover, explicitly does not mean the summation of individuals' private wants. It means the good of the community as a whole. Defining the good as the maximum satisfaction of individual preferences is simple utilitarianism, the "hedonic calculus."[97]

Thinking in *this* mode we may well have some doubts about trusting environmental matters entirely to the wisdom of private interests. Private owners may well choose to make money by running a resource down or exhausting it, especially if, as is quite simple in our economy, they can take their capital gains elsewhere to invest in another project: take the profit and run. If market price were the only way to express value, wetlands everywhere would be drained for buildings, even if there were a scientific consensus that their preservation was ecologically essential.

Making market price the effective determinant of social value has the further drawback of depriving people without purchasing power of any voice in those decisions that will affect the environment in which they have to live. The redress they are sometimes offered in the literature of free market environmentalism, that they can sue for damages anyone whose activities hurt them, is not much more than a bad joke. People with little money can never afford to sue a well-lawyered corporation; and even if collectively they could, in a class-action suit, using the court system to control environmental depredation must be just about the most costly, cumbersome, inconsistent, and haphazard way of accomplishing the job. It is little wonder that Loren Wilkinson and colleagues conclude, "The price system can never, by itself, be adequate to the stewardly task of earthkeeping."[98]

It appears that the common good must often be defended *against* private interests; and in those cases the appropriate route is surely to pass through the legitimate political process, one which incorporates all voices equitably and probably equally—in other words, by democratic decision-making. Ownership and property rights (even if justly acquired) are not absolute in Christian tradition, but must be qualified by just use. There is thus ethical justification for a properly representative government to define the common good and further it by devices like zoning laws, tax incentives, and even, if sparingly used, direct regulation.

The tension between these two goods, personal freedom and the common good, must be regarded as permanent, even if it can be argued that to some extent the latter serves also the former. I would tilt toward freedom and place the burden of proof on those who would deny it for the sake of the common good. But at the same time I acknowledge the obvious, that there are times when personal desires must yield to the community. Private persons can be asked, as a matter of law and ethics, to have due regard for the public good even at the expense of their selfish interests.

Of course it is simple ethical realism to know that appeal to the common welfare is not enough by itself. Making economic individualism the practical norm in matters environmental may well be what is necessary "under the conditions of sin," harnessing the power of self-interest for more inclusive goals. According to one pessimistic assessment, moral suasion on environmental matters moves no more than 5 percent of our people, so economic incentives are clearly needed to get the job done.[99] But at the same time Christians cannot cynically discard the appeal to selflessness. Other-regarding love is, after all, the Christian behavioral norm, however imperfectly we sinful people realize it. If we are to make stewardship of the gifts of God our guiding principle here, it seems clear enough that we are called to think beyond self-interest.

IV

Another aspect of environmental politics which is worthy of thorough attention from Christians is the relation between environmentalism and justice. The subject is complex and deserves the extended treatment it has been receiving from many sources. Let us simply note and summarize here some of the salient points in the debate.

Although it is probably not the place where most people would begin this discussion, and is a late-comer to the ethical literature,[100] the obligation to future generations is one of those foundational notions that affect all of environmental thought. Environmentalism is mostly about slow changes over long periods of time, and thus necessarily must consider conditions that will exist well after we ourselves have died. Do we owe anything to those who will live then? Why should we plan for a future we will not see, indeed one whose needs we can scarcely imagine?

There are those who argue reasonably enough that we have no such obligation. We owe something to those who have given us our lives, our forebears; but they are gone, and there is no way to repay them. We do not discharge that debt by paying someone else, our descendants. Posterity has not done anything for us, and we thus owe it nothing. Anything we bequeath to the future is a pure gift, a free will offering. Moreover, even if we were moved by generosity, we could not know what those who come after us, especially those who come *long* after us, will really need, what their lives will be like, and what ways they will have of managing their environment. We would not know what to do now to accommodate an unknown future. To get a sense of the difficulty we have only to ask ourselves what those of a century ago, or two (let alone longer) could have even guessed about our lives today.

On the other hand we might argue that we all know we are responsible for the consequences of our actions, and that our debts outlive us (our estates must pay them off). It is common sense to say that if we engage in wasteful and destructive behavior, but escape the consequences of our actions by passing them off on future generations, we have done something morally wrong. We know we would be guilty, even if we were not alive to face our victims. Nor can we hide behind ignorance of the needs of coming centuries. Biological similarity assures their comparable need for air, food, water, space, and shelter; and we know enough ecology to admit that what we do now will affect our descendants' ability to satisfy those needs. Thus even if we do not know the details, we do know we have an obligation to take future generations into account.

We may work thus on a "naturalistic" level to establish our responsibilities, and secular philosophers continue to do so with greater or less success. But here is a case, it seems to me, where Christians can contribute something immensely important from the resources of faith, something not available to the secular mind. The argument begins with our answerability to a God who stands beyond the processes of nature and history. From this theological "fact" alone we learn that we are responsible for our actions for as long as they have consequences. To love a God whose providence embraces generations past and yet to come must move us more powerfully to environmental responsibility than simple rational reflections on the nature of debt and repayment.

Biblical theology appeals explicitly to this general insight with its assumption of intergenerational solidarity, the obligation to pass on to subsequent generations the divine blessing given "to [our] descendants forever."[101] Christians appeal to it also in the doctrine of the communion of saints, where all the faithful, living, departed, and yet to come, are bound together in Christ, virtually present to each other in living relationship. Christian love is not limited to the near and familiar, but is given to all the household of God, to all people in all time.

Thus our duty to future generations is real, even if we cannot predict in much detail what they will need. Admittedly the area of our ignorance is indeed vast, considering the rapidity and extent of technological change; and for that reason in cases of genuine conflict between present and future peoples I would prefer the present, whose needs we know, to the future with its uncertainties. It would, for example, surely be impossible to use the Christian ethic, with its spontaneity and immediacy in addressing human need, *against* the poor and the miserable among us, even if someone should claim that the increase in their numbers threatens future quality of life. How could Christians ever say they were not called to feed the hungry and clothe the naked?

And yet, although "priority to the present" is for that reason a defensible maxim, human needs and our responsibility to meet them do transcend our own lives. Our policies must keep the far future in mind. "Sustainability" is thus a decent watchword, provided it is employed with due humility about our knowledge of future needs. Perhaps the best gift we can bequeath to our descendants is our high technology and the knowledge base to keep it developing, as the best insurance against future environmental disaster.

We can employ that same logic, that technological knowledge combined with ecological commitment will show the way to a livable future, to another thorny problem in environmental justice, the development of poor nations. It must be said in all honesty that "third world" (a term increasingly obsolete) aspirations for economic development to escape from poverty have run headlong into environmentalists who think the "crisis" can be traced, in all its forms, to industrial civilization. Development, they say, cannot be as it was in the wealthy nations. That is physically impossible now, given the scarcity of resources, and in any event hasn't brought the industrial world a good life. The program of "bioregionalism" advanced by some environmentalists, which would require a kind of local self-sufficiency instead of participation in the global economy, would certainly mean a lesser standard of living; and it is meant to, since a rising standard is held to mean dangerously growing resource consumption. But bioregionalism would also put a real crimp in the development hopes of the poor nations, leaving them to fend for themselves without our help or even our concern.[102]

Peoples of the poorer regions are well aware of this bias against them. Restricting development for the sake of a supposed planetary environmental good is bound to look like an attempt of the affluent to keep their comforts to themselves. Brazil, for example, when criticized for allowing the cutting of its rain forest, wonders aloud why it should be prohibited from doing what wealthier nations have already done in the course of their own development. Does this external pressure amount to interference in its domestic affairs, "neo-colonialism" with an environmental twist? Small wonder that when the United Nations first tried to interest developing countries in ecology, it met fierce resistance to environmentalism as a Western plot to keep the third world subjugated. And so the U.N. has mounted its program with two foci instead of one, "environment *and* development," as in the title of the Rio conference. The U.N. environmental agency was placed in Nairobi for the same reason, to show the third world their concerns would not be forgotten.

Among environmentalists more politically to the Left, the solution to the development problem is apt to be some sort of redistribution of wealth, or "de-development" of the industrial world, since, they insist, more wealth cannot be created without unacceptable ecological damage.[103] Christian writers in this vein back up their argument with a stiff evocation of the biblical warnings to the rich and our obligation to the poor—salutary, correct, always worth taking to heart, I have no doubt. I talk that way, too, and I mean it. But it may not be a relevant response to the environmental problem, such as it is. The trouble is not simply the political unlikelihood of a major wealth transfer. The difficulty is the economic thesis that we are rich at the expense of the poor. It assumes a zero-sum game. But this is almost certainly not true, for there are patterns of development that can raise everyone's living standards.

Here we come to a more moderate and realistic position. Let us assume, as a Christian imperative, our obligation to assist the economic development of the world's poor, and to encourage trade and lending arrangements to facilitate this process. And then let us resolve to use our science, our technology, and our political will to translate this imperative into an ecologically sound reality.[104] The process will not be simple, and we should be prepared to accept some environmental trade-offs. It is probably too optimistic to think that rising living standards will not have at least some negative impacts on third world environments, too optimistic to think these countries can lift themselves out of poverty without a course of development which for a while at least entails practices ecologists will not like.[105] But proceeding intelligently and cautiously we can minimize these effects without sacrificing our commitment to human welfare.

The reigning mantra for this program is "sustainable development." As a slogan it does have a whiff of the oxymoron about it, a suspicion of a political correctness designed to satisfy both environmentalists and the least developed nations by combining incompatibles.[106] The trick is to get beyond this marriage of convenience to realistic policies. It can be done. Recall that the existing environment of poor countries is hardly pristine but bedeviled by pre-industrial pollution; that rising living standards in many ways help such conditions, because nations with the wherewithal to make environmental improvements choose to do so; and that new technologies mean that development need not, and will not, follow the pattern of the currently industrialized nations.

When we choose to support new policies that affect development, we will want to favor, as a matter of Christian conscience, those that protect the interests of the weak. The gross neglect at Rio of the third world's air and water pollution, in favor of a disputed focus on the alleged greenhouse effect, is an example of a place where critical Christian voices should have been heard. Another possible example is the banning of DDT in tropical Africa, where it is the most effective weapon against malaria. Another is any conservationist land-use policy that makes it harder to grow the food needed to alleviate world hunger.

The road ahead is littered with such ethical land mines. Debt-for-nature swaps can easily be seen as taking advantage of a country's economic weakness to force internal policy changes which its own citizens do not want. Promoting "ecotourism" as a way to save endangered natural areas no doubt adds to the economic uses which can save such lands, but the economically advanced nations had best be careful not to champion a policy whereby the poorer regions are denied development so that they can serve as rest and recreation areas for tourists from the wealthier parts of the planet.

A particularly painful illustration of this problem of development and justice is the population issue, here again functioning as a sort of bellwether of environmentalism. Many Western ecologists are on record as saying that the less-developed part of the world cannot possibly grow economically until it shrinks demographically. Even if they have their facts right, an arguable point as noted earlier, they are faulted and feared in the developing countries because their programs, if actually adopted by governments, can lead to serious violations of human rights. This has already happened in India, where forced sterilization failed and was largely responsible for the fall of Indira Gandhi's government, and China, where well-publicized abuses include forced abortions and female infanticide. In Bangladesh an incentive system for sterilizations verged on the compulsory, given the desperation of people who agreed to be sterilized for cash payments.

The truth is that a lower birth rate depends a good deal on a *prior* improvement in socio-economic conditions. Otherwise women will have more children because they want them, because they need them for security, because they have to have many to make sure that some will live past infancy. And if the material conditions of life are not improved, millions will continue to suffer anyway, whether birth rates decline or not, since numbers are not the principal cause of current malnutrition and other ills.

Beyond their misunderstanding of the facts, beyond their tolerance of draconian solutions, the controllers are finally accused of regarding people, at least when found in great numbers, as a kind of pollution. There is among them that dreadful elitist assumption of the wealthy and comfortable that lesser lives are not worth living. There is more than a touch of "first world" imperialism here, and it may explain why environmentalists are more excited about habitat and species protection than about human health in the poor nations: the human species is not endangered, and could use a little thinning out.

I am aware of the seriousness of this charge, and I do not make it lightly. This attitude can indeed be found in many population crisis writings. The purest example I know is Garrett Hardin's pseudo-scientific fable *Exploring New Ethics for Survival*, written around his earlier famous essay "The Tragedy of the Commons." He imagines a large spaceship, three kilometers across, sent out from Earth to find new worlds to colonize. It is peopled by innocent earthlings who are unaware of a ruling elite of twenty wise people hidden in a glass mountain in the middle of the ship. Naturally, since this a demographic fable about the exhaustion of the earth's "commons," the earthlings cannot control their population growth; and, through many a heavy-handed metaphor, Hardin tells us what must be done: the wise controllers must kill them. He tries to soften our natural ethical revulsion by describing the teeming earthlings in subhuman language, which of course only makes the lesson of this grotesque tale even less palatable: we have here *untermenschen*, and the *endlösung*, the "final solution" to the problem of people and resources, is confronting us.[107]

Christian environmentalists are obviously not about to have anything to do with attitudes like Hardin's. But we will have to ask ourselves honestly how we propose to solve the conflict between ecological concerns and the hopes of the poor for a better life. There are those whose solution is to deny that the conflict exists. Seeking a way to honor the poor nations' justifiable drive for economic development while at the same time restraining industrial assaults on the environment, and confronted with an embarrassing domestic analogue in the historic locus of environmentalism among the comfortable classes, they simply assert, often without any argumentation whatever, that justice and sound ecology imply and require each other. The two are joined by yet another coined "eco-" word, "eco-justice," which implies their unity. "Justice, equality, and peace are intimately tied with ecological stability. Recognition of nature's harmony and action to maintain it are preconditions for distributive justice." "We affirm, in the strongest possible terms, the indivisibility of social justice and the preservation of the environment."[108]

"Ecojustice" probably ought to have meant justice for nature, on the assumption that nature has rights, but was used instead to mean something quite different, something really *not* biocentric, the idea that sound ecology would serve justice among people. When the wealthy use a disproportionate amount of the earth's resources at the expense of the poor, they offend against "ecojustice." Using up the planet's riches now instead of leaving something for future generations is another example. So are ecological assaults on the places where the poor and powerless live, e.g. siting toxic dumps in their neighborhoods, or displacing them to build highways—the infamous "NIMBY" syndrome, "not in my backyard," which operates to preserve the amenities and property values of the middle and upper classes.

If we define "ecojustice" very broadly, "justice in our use of creation," then we might actually extend its meaning to include the animal rights movement and biocentrism, as in the harmony of humans and nature in the biblical vision of the peaceable kingdom.[109] But this extension strikes me as a bit of a stretch, for reasons given earlier, and because the true instances of "injustice" cited in the prophetic literature focus on human oppression of other humans. Justice, like rights, is an intrahuman concept. But even without this extension, "ecojustice" casts a wide net.

When advocates of the term do explain the unity they proclaim between ecology and justice, they are likely to argue that the mentality of domination is the link. Domination of nature is tied to social domination. Get rid of the first and the second will fall also; or, put differently, the first led inevitably to the second. "An ecological ethic must always be an ethic of eco-justice which recognizes the interconnection of social domination and domination of nature."[110] The World Council of Churches' study theme, "Justice, Peace, and the Integrity of Creation," implies that preserving the "integrity" of creation means a nonexploitive lifestyle which will inevitably redound to the good of the poor—the limited-resources, zero-sum-game argument about development again. The theme also implies an organic unity of all aspects of life in some vague and ill-defined way, thought of as a basically ecological way of thinking: everything connected to every-thing else.

A moment's reflection ought to dispel such reasoning. "Dominat-ing" nature (like gardening) is clearly not the same thing as "domi-nating" human beings (like wars of conquest). One is morally positive, the other negative, and we all know which is which. The "integrity of creation," a curious and dubious concept anyway given the earth's dramatic variability over geological time, has little or nothing to do with the way people treat each other. The truth is that sound ecology and the practice of justice are different concepts. Where they conflict, as in "NIMBY" arguments, we do not have a phenomenon that requires a catchy new word to understand it, but rather, alas and to our shame, yet another instance of the indignities visited upon the powerless. The solution to such problems is not to assert blandly that adopting optimally sound environmental practices will automatically redound to the material well-being of the poor, but to admit that that might well not be the case, and then to find a way to share the benefits and burdens equitably. Conflicts and trade-offs can-not be wished away with slogans, but must be honestly faced.

In short and in sum, the Christian pursuit of justice within the constraints of sound environmental policy will have to be in the first instance very practical, with common sense, science, and economics as our conceptual tools. Stewardship of the earth cannot be respon-sibly practiced without them. We will have to admit that some environmental ideals, like the recovery of pre-industrial purity or the restoration of much of the wild land now converted to agriculture, cannot be done without unacceptable harm to people. We must find a way to respond to the aspirations of the poor of the world, using our technical knowledge to control whatever environmental harm we might have to accept in the process. We will also have to admit that some of our practices do cause real ecological damage, and that in our own interests we must find a way to curb them, recognizing that some sacrifices will be necessary, and seeking to distribute them fairly, with a pronounced bias toward the interests of the weak.

Exactly how these principles will play out in specific decisions, just how the balances here required can be struck, is a matter for practical judgment, for reason and science, for trial and error. But we are smart enough to do the job, armed not only with our natural God-given intelligence, but also with the sound theological realism of Christian faith. Avoiding both environmental apocalypticism and technological naiveté, succumbing neither to undue pessimism nor utopian idealism, we will engage these new challenges soberly, seeking always human salvation over misery, death, and destruction.

Fatalism, Hope, and Courage

The original Christian humanists of the sixteenth century loved learning and found that it enriched their faith. Men like Erasmus and Reuchlin did not shrink from the new, and newly recovered, knowledge of their day, but embraced it and celebrated the achievements of human culture. It is appropriate in our day to recall them, and in particular to apply their enthusiasm to the natural sciences, the perpetually "new" knowledge of modern culture.

This is not, however, the reigning attitude in the environmental movement, which feeds on a sense of a crisis allegedly induced by modern scientific and technological culture, and whose prophets have repeatedly warned us against hoping for a "fix" from the same source that has caused the crisis. The movement is, in that sense, "anti-humanistic." It despises the pass to which human ingenuity has brought us, and in some quarters goes so far as to suggest that the root of the problem is the human presence itself. Clever demons, we are on the edge of destroying life on earth; and earth would plainly be better off without us.

This anti-humanism is barely submerged in environmental writing and pops out regularly. Thus animal rights advocate Stephen R. L. Clark: "What I detest is humanism," because it sets us off from non-human creatures whom we then exploit. "There is no depth of self-serving stupidity to which mankind cannot sink. . . . Men's hearts are evil from the beginning." Human personality and civilization "seem frankly psychopathic." Ecofeminist Rosemary Ruether calls humankind "the rogue elephant of nature," more dangerous to planetary health than any other species. Biocentrist Paul Taylor says that as members of a biotic community we must be impartial toward all species, our own included, that in fact we are unnecessary to other species who would be helped by our extinction. Ecological theologian Thomas Berry is similarly minded: "The human species has, for some thousands of years, shown itself to be a pernicious presence in the world of the living on a unique and universal scale." Evolutionary biologist E. O. Wilson says it was a "misfortune for the living world" that a carnivorous primate—humans—made the evolutionary break-through and came to dominate. "Darwin's dice have rolled badly for Earth."[111]

Extreme though these citations sound, they are the expressions of an attitude made all but inevitable by the attack of environmental philosophers on anthropocentrism. Focussing on the "biotic commu-nity" or the "whole planet Earth," or "Gaia" as the locus of primary value reduces the importance of humanity to the same level as other creatures; and it is a very small step beyond that, a step all too often taken, to say that humans are *less* valuable to the whole than others creatures, indeed actually dangerous.

This devaluation of the human does make some other environ-mentalists nervous. Clearly it risks sacrificing individual goods, per-haps even some individual lives, to the health of a higher planetary good. Most seem to hope that humanity will not be harmed by a stress on the value of the biotic whole, but will actually find its life improved and its long-term survival prospects enhanced. But a readiness to subordinate human good is required by the general principles of biocentrism, deep ecology, ecofeminism, and the animal rights movement, individually and collectively.

A key element in this devaluation of the human is fatalism. Biocentrists take their cues as to what ought to be from what is, and thus their views of an acceptable future from what will happen if we let the natural world follow its own laws as far as possible. If an organism exists, the biocentrist presumes it has an important ecologi-cal niche and should be left alone. "Natural kinds are good kinds until proven otherwise."[112] If it is an ecological misfit it will perish naturally anyway and we should not regret its demise. Death may be bad for individuals, but it is good for the system.

The whole direction of biocentric thought is to apply this ecologi-cal "wisdom," if that is the word, to *all* species, including *homo sapiens*. Because the consequences of this conclusion are so fearsome for most peoples' sensitivities, it is hard to find candid public acknowledg-ment of it among its believers. When the truth does come out, ordinary ethical opinion, unenlightened by this new environmental realism, is apt to be appalled. Should we curtail medicine so that more of us may die "naturally" and earlier? Yes. Should we refrain from feeding the hungry, so that population will not exceed its

boundaries? Yes, said the "lifeboat school," and especially its helms-
man Garrett Hardin, whose bluntness ought to be an embarrassment
to the current generation of biocentrists. Or consider Callicott's
rendering of William Aiken's questions as direct statements: "Massive human diebacks would be good. It is our duty to cause them. It
is our species duty, relative to the whole, to eliminate 90 percent of
our numbers."[113]

Even Lynn White, that most humane and Christian man, walked
up to the edge of this moral abyss. Humans are crowding out earth's
other species, our "comrades" on the planet, and a balance needs to
be restored. How shall we do this? Shall individual human beings be
sacrificed, in defiance of traditional Christian ethics, if some killing
will save many species? White hesitated, he said, to "light candles
before the saints requesting a new Black Death" to give us, like
fourteenth-century Europe before us, a "tragic respite" from our
ecological peril. Almost visibly he drew back from the fearful answer;
and yet with only slight obliqueness he said it: Many must die.[114]

To be sure, and to be fair, many biocentrists recoil from the social
implications of their theory. It is only the biocentric egalitarians, for
whom all life is of equal value, who admit that they are driven to
these fearful anti-human conclusions. For the others, their schema of
hierarchical differentiation allow them to claim a different level of
moral behavior among humans, different from that between humans
and the natural world, and certainly different from natural amorality.
Callicott insists that "humanitarian obligations in general come before environmental duties." Rolston calls it "monstrous" not to feed
starving humans, though he would let overpopulated wild herds
die.

But the boundaries between nature and culture are blurred and
repeatedly crossed, as the examples of White and Hardin show well
enough. Callicott acknowledges that the conflicts are a "difficult and
delicate question." Nash calls them "immensely complicated."
Wilkinson speaks of having to make "difficult choices between the
good of human and non-human creatures with care, wisdom, and a
willingness to feel the pain we inflict on fellow creatures." Johnson
admits that weighing competing interests is "a very difficult matter,"
"a matter of cases, varying from one species to the next, and perhaps
varying among individuals as well." "It is not at all clear where the
final line is to be drawn."

Paul Taylor, stung by the charge that he can't distinguish between killing humans and swatting flies, is not terribly consoling when he defends himself with a depends-on-the-situation argument: All killing requires moral justification, since the inherent worth of all creatures is equal; e.g. it would be more wrong to kill a rare wildflower than to kill a human in self-defense. Rolston says that ecological "fitness" means and implies different things in nature than it does for humans, but (let the reader beware) they have similarity, too; they are "homologous" or "analogous." "This biological world that *is* also *ought* to be; we must argue from the natural to the moral . . . So much the worse for those humanistic ethics no longer functioning in, nor suited to, their changing environment."[115] Apparently one can, in a way, import ethics from nature to culture.

And that is precisely the ethical problem. Without a secure anchor in humanism—and I will say really *Christian* humanism, where the special human place in nature is theologically protected—without that, biocentrism risks great moral evils. At the extreme it appears actually indifferent to human destiny. Our eventual demise, although hastened by our environmentally harmful lifestyle, is in any case inevitable, and because inevitable, ought to be accepted. Since species must be allowed their "evolutionary time" and then die, and because this process is "good," the human species, too, must expect to perish; and from nature's point of view, that will be normal. If nature were capable of regret, there would not be any for our passing. The ecosystem will survive as well or better without us at the top of the food chain. But since nature is amoral, we must say that our extinction is of no moral significance in nature.

Would God care? The whole direction of our faith says that God would indeed care, which suggests strongly that we should oppose biocentrism and not anticipate our species' demise with evolutionary equanimity. That would not be an outcome compatible with the Judeo-Christian tradition. No one will deny our mortality ("You are dust, and to dust you shall return"), but neither will any Christian or Jew deny the special significance of humanity ("So God created man in his own image, . . . male and female he created them"). I admit that this is a conviction of faith. What God really is about is not accessible to us, and I would not dare to say I knew, although, as I will say in a moment, I believe we have a theologically-legitimated hope.

Whether such modesty is becoming or not, it eludes the biocentrists, who seem to know more than I do about the ultimate principles which rule the universe. Here, for example, is Carol Christ:

> We are no more valuable to the life of the universe than a field [of flowers]. . . . The divinity that shapes our ends is an impersonal process of life, death, and transformation. . . . The life force does not care more about human creativity and choice than it cares about the ability . . . of moss to form on the side of a tree. The human species, like other species, might in time become extinct, dying so that other lives might live.[116]

Rolston is only moderately more hopeful: The evolutionary system is "not just a random walk" but "some kind of steady, if statistical heading." In the extinction of some species and the appearance of new ones "a hidden principle seems to be at work, organizing the cosmos in a coherent way." But that is scant comfort to humans, who come very late to the story and are only "short-sighted and arrogant" if they think it was meant for them. He is quite fatalistic about our destiny: recognizing that there is nothing necessary or inevitable about our appearance on earth, we will simply have to accept the overall course of evolution as good, no matter where it eventually goes.[117]

James Gustafson, a justly celebrated ethicist, has written similarly that we should not count on humanity's being at the apex of creation nor consider that human good trumps the good of non-human nature. Our disappearance would not be bad "from a theocentric perspective," which acknowledges that "the source and power and order of all of nature is not always beneficent in its outcomes for the diversity of life and for the well-being of humans as part of that." "The Divine . . . [is] the ultimate source of all human good, but does not guarantee it." Such ruminations have led Nash to characterize Gustafson's "God" as

> . . . a nonconscious and nonmoral ordering power without intention, volition, or cognition. . . . This power sustains the universe, apparently unintentionally, but lacks the purposive, benevolent, or redemptive qualities to seek the good of individuals, the human species, otherkind, or the whole cosmos . . . This perspective seems close to atheism or pantheism.[118]

The ecological ethic emerging from biocentric fatalism, such as it is, is simply to enjoy the earth's fecundity, to laugh and weep and celebrate all life, whether it is our life or not. "Humanity's highest possibility is to bear witness to and participate in the great process of life itself."[119] And so the biocentrist love affair with a mysterious

Natural Process cultivates, inevitably, indifference to the human prospect.

It is, of course, a bit odd for biocentrists to view humanity as just another species serving out its evolutionary time, when with the same voice they must also acknowledge that we are a very special species, endowed with enormous power over the environment. We cannot renounce this power, either. It is ours to use for good or ill, and so they urge us to use it in a self-limiting way to preserve the rest of the environment and to care for the other creatures of the earth. Notice that the message is anthropocentric in spite of itself: Our great power engenders our great responsibility. But that, of course, is precisely the Christian ethic of dominion and stewardship. We return, naturally, inevitably, to Christian humanism: made in the divine image, dramatically dominant over the rest of life, it is our God-given task to be responsible caretakers of the Creator's handiwork.

Those who wish to deny the centrality of humanity have to reject this religious conception, and even reject the religion which brought it forth. For these critics it is arrogance to think of ourselves as the special object of divine creation. Perhaps, in an attempt to mollify them, we may put it more modestly and say that as humans we can only see creation through our humanity. We cannot, of course, know what God's ultimate purposes are; but we can know, by a faith which is confirmed by common sense, that we are special among creatures in our capacities and thus in our responsibilities, including our responsibilities for the earth and its lesser creatures.

Ultimately, however we express the point, there seems to be no reasonable, morally defensible way to proceed except by using human welfare as our compass heading. Yes, this is an anthropocentric prescription. It is inescapable. Attempts to mute it or compromise, like Brian Norton's distinction between weak and strong anthropocentrism, do not really succeed in softening the humanistic choice which has been made. Norton tells us that "strong anthropocentrism" means heedless consumption of resources, whereas the "weak" version, which he defends, means acceding to a rational worldview in which the environment is managed for human survival. Not truly a compromise, much less a resolution of the biocentrist challenge, Norton's view may be reduced, I think, to the "wise-use" environmental ethic, smart anthropocentrism.[120]

And smart it must be. It is appropriate, in the spirit of Christian humanism, to say a final word in favor of human intelligence. The devaluation of reason and science is more likely to doom us than to lead us back to paradise. Life was once short, prey to disease, starvation, and natural disaster. It still is in some places, and could become so everywhere again, especially if we really do accept the prescriptions of the radical biocentrists and recover a primitive lifestyle. Rather than abandon our wits and throw ourselves on the dubious mercy of Mother Nature, it seems a lot more promising to use our brains to save ourselves as best we can, one problem at a time, through trial and error. This is a tentative, modest but more likely proposal than a wholesale "paradigm shift" to a new ideology, abandoning what we know for a blank future with an impersonal biosphere evolving randomly without any particular affection for human beings. Anathema though it surely is to biocentrists, deep ecologists, ecofeminists and their like, one and all, to say so, it is far more likely that our environmental problems will yield to science and smart management than they will to a quasi-mystical, neo-pagan, prescientific reenchantment of the world.

I do not know where the human story will end. No one does. Natural history affords us very uncertain and not altogether comforting clues. Nature has changed rather dramatically through the long geological ages. Students of evolution have noted the underlying instability of natural processes, that relatively sudden inexplicable, unforeseeable changes have doomed whole species—and that it could happen to us, too, just as the emergence of *homo sapiens* in the first place could be counted a mere accident, at least as far as we can tell from studying nature alone. Even those of us whose faith permits us to find teleological wisdom in the long process would have to guess that the Creator intends something other than natural stasis.

In view of the apparent long-term precariousness of our existence, it is little wonder that people without a religious anchor tend to pessimism. Thus the philosopher Bertrand Russell, convinced that the universe is "purposeless, void of meaning," that the human race is "the product of causes which had no prevision of the end they were achieving . . . the outcome of accidental collections of atoms . . ." and that all the glorious achievements of civilization "are destined to extinction in the vast death of the solar system . . . buried beneath the debris of a universe in ruins," concludes, "Brief and powerless is Man's life; on him and all his race the slow, sure doom falls pitiless and dark. . . . For Man . . . it remains only to cherish . . . the lofty thoughts that ennoble his little day."[121]

The economist Robert Heilbroner, asking "Is there hope for man?" answers, basing his pessimism principally on environmental deterioration and human inflexibility:

> The outlook for man, I believe, is painful, difficult, perhaps desperate, and the hope that can be held out for his future prospect seems to be very slim indeed. . . . The answer to whether we can conceive the future other than as a continuation of the darkness, cruelty, and disorder of the past seems to me to be no; and to the question of whether worse impends, yes.[122]

But let us turn instead to a more hopeful vision, the defiant humanism of William Faulkner's address accepting the Nobel prize for literature:

> I decline to accept the end of man. It is easy enough to say that man is immortal simply because he will endure: that when the last ding-dong of doom has clanged and faded from the last worthless rock hanging tideless in the last red and dying evening, that even then there will be one more sound: that of his puny, inexhaustible voice, still talking. I refuse to accept this. I believe that man will not merely endure: he will prevail. He is immortal, not because he alone among creatures has an inexhaustible voice, but because he has a soul, a spirit capable of compassion and sacrifice and endurance.[123]

Perhaps Faulkner was whistling past the graveyard, but Christians may confidently welcome his courage and his hope and go on to ground them in the goodness and mercy of God. From beginning to end the Bible breathes the spirit of trust and hope in God. "Thou, O Lord, art my hope, my trust," sings the Psalmist. "The eye of the Lord is . . . on those who hope in his steadfast love." The New Testament has an especially rich and developed doctrine of hope, the "hope of sharing the glory of God," the hope which "does not disappoint us, because God's love has been poured into our hearts through the Holy Spirit," the hope which together with faith and love is the abiding tripartite foundation of the Christian life, the "hope set on the living God" which is the reason for our toiling and striving, the "hope of the Gospel" from which we are not to stray, the hope of which we are to give an account whenever asked.[124]

Trusting, then, in the promises of God, and living in the blessing of redemption offered to humankind, Christians ought to work confidently toward the future, bending their efforts above all to perpetuating human life. That goal ought to be the overriding test of our ecological conduct. In arguing otherwise, large sections of the environmental movement are on the wrong track. In the name of its own humanistic faith Christianity ought to criticize it, rather than scramble to say, "Me, too." Our survival does not depend on new paradigms, with new ethics, whether they are based on archaic, pre-Christian immersion in nature or on the alleged imperatives of new environmental science. What is historic and traditional in our valuation of Creation is a perfectly sufficient guide to sound ecology. What is required of discipleship is to live out that valuation actively and faithfully.

Chapter 2

In Flagrant Dissent:
An Environmentalist's Contentions

James A. Nash

I was offered the alternative of responding critically to Derr's primary essay, or constructing my contrary position. I chose the former, partly because I have developed my own stance somewhat extensively elsewhere,[1] and partly because I am convinced that Derr's position must not stand unchallenged! It represents a widespread and unwarranted distortion of much environmental thought. It demands to be faced and refuted, if for no other reason than to reduce the prospect that this viewpoint will gain adherents or repute. My prime regret is that I have too little time and space to note all my points of disagreement with Derr's text. I also regret that I cannot respond to the other author of this book, Richard John Neuhaus, with whom, if his previous work[2] is a reliable guide, I am also in substantial disagreement.

I am by no means in total contention with Derr. I agree with some of his grievances about contemporary environmental thought. For instance, I share his antagonism to what I've described as the "ecological complaint against Christianity," namely, that the Christian faith is the primary culprit in the ecological crisis.[3] That is truly "historical nonsense," as Derr argues—indeed, anthropological and logical nonsense as well, in light of the cultural and religious miscomparisons that are usually associated with this complaint. Fortunately, this complaint has been subsiding recently, partly as a consequence of the critical responses of some Christian theologians and ethicists (including Derr as a significant contributor), as well as the increased involvement of Christians in ecological causes.

I agree also with much of Derr's reaction to romantic views of nature—for example, sentimental illusions about harmony and peace. Still, Derr overreacts and fails to see the full ambiguities, including the positive and creative possibilities in human relationships with the rest of nature. Part, but only part, of the human condition is the struggle against the rest of nature for human survival and cultural thriving. Some "subduing" is necessary. The ecological crisis, however, is subduing far beyond the point of necessity and equity. We can still justify "loving nature," as I do, but it must be an interpretation of Christian love that is grounded in ecological realism, not the romanticism that Derr rightly rebukes.

Finally, I agree with some of the criticisms that Derr makes of particular environmental interpreters—including Lynn White, Jr., Garrett Hardin, Paul Shephard, Thomas Berry, Carol Christ, Paul Ehrlich, E. O. Wilson, and Peter Singer, although I am not convinced that Derr is always fair to them. "Extreme" expressions or perspectives of particular individuals are sometimes cited as typical examples of their work or even of a whole movement. Ridicule and caricature sometimes substitute for argument. His criticisms of the work of Holmes Rolston, for example, oversimplify a sophisticated body of thought.

Despite some areas of agreement with Derr, I, of course, have some fundamental disagreements. These I will explore in seven categories: (1) stewardship, (2) theological foundations, (3) intrinsic value, (4) biotic rights, (5) ecofeminism, (6) environmental policies, and (7) the social consequences of biocentrism.[4]

Lest the blunt character of my critique in these pages leave any doubt, I count myself as a grateful friend and an intellectual beneficiary of Tom Derr. He is always a formidable thinker and dialogue partner. One can always count on him to be clear, candid, creative, and provocative. Indeed, in this case, he has provoked me mightily. I will respond accordingly, but not without the appreciation and affection I feel. So, having abandoned nearly all hope of converting him, I will seek to demolish his arguments—lovingly, I hope.

Stewardship

Derr emphatically states that "the real, orthodox Christian attitude toward nature" is stewardship or trusteeship to God, the ultimate proprietor. Derr never adequately defines or interprets the concept which is central to his ethic, but it is still clear that stewardship means the use and management of the rest of nature solely for human sustainability. Nature's value, he claims, is strictly instrumental for human values. He sees the stewardship model now being replaced by "the increasingly powerful and pervasive school" of biocentrism, of which nearly all its diverse members view stewardship as "repulsively anthropocentric."

My contention with Derr and others is not about the centrality of stewardship for Christian ecological ethics, but rather about their exclusively humanistic and instrumentalist interpretations of stewardship. In some settings, I have been reluctant to use the concept of stewardship to describe human ecological responsibilities precisely because of the contradictory interpretations on the current scene. A main debate about stewardship is whether it means loving care and service for the sake of both humans and other lifeforms, or the technical management of the biosphere as nothing more than a "resource base" for human needs and wants. If stewardship means the former, as I think it does in many historical and modern Christian interpretations, then I happily accept it. If, however, it means the latter, as it does in the dominant cultural ethos, which Derr seems to reflect, then I must reject it. Stewardship in the former sense is quite compatible with the inclusion of values for otherkind. Douglas John Hall[5] and Loren Wilkinson and colleagues[6]—whose works Derr commends as prime models of the stewardship he defends—interpret stewardship as loving service in relationships with all God's creatures.

Theological Foundations

Derr claims that the theological concept of cosmic redemption "cannot tell us much about the care of nature beyond what we already know from our stewardship obligation, that we are to preserve this world as habitat fit for humanity." He suggests that the same is true of other Christian affirmations. Only the divine-human relationship counts ethically for Derr. He writes as if humans are not parts and products of nature, as if we have not evolved in interaction with all other creatures and elements, as if we are an ecologically segregated species designed mainly for managerial mastery over the rest of nature—indeed, as if the realities of biological kinship and ecological interdependence with all kind are irrelevant for theological reflection and moral responsibility. In a simple assertion, he sums up his theology of nature: "Nature is made for us, as we are made for God." In response, I repeat a line I wrote in a recent essay: "The traditional idea that the earth, or even the universe, was created solely for humans is, in our scientific age, sinfully arrogant, biologically naive, cosmologically silly, and therefore theologically indefensible."[7]

Contrary to Derr, the central affirmations of the Christian church imply a great deal beyond his interpretations of stewardship. Respect for the intrinsic value of nonhuman life is coherent with basic Christian theological themes—indeed, to a far fuller degree than any competing interpretations of ecological responsibilities. I can only suggest the general lines of this argument here, but I have developed the point at length on several key doctrines in my *Loving Nature*.[8]

In the doctrine of creation, the Crafter who is Love has made all creatures as acts of love and as recipients of ongoing love, endowing all life with a moral status, and uniting all life in a theocentric and biological bond. In Genesis 1, the creation and its creatures are declared to be "good" *before* the emergence of *Homo sapiens*. In Psalm 104, God is praised for comprehensive benevolence to all creatures, *independent of* any human benefits. God values the whole creation *apart from* any human utility in Job 38-41. The logic of universal providence implies that the Creator is concerned about the well-being of the whole creation and all its parts, not only with the human component. Ethically, since fidelity to God implies loyalty to divine valuations and affections, we are called to image the values of the ultimate Valuer—indeed, to mirror the love of Christ toward all God's beloved, not only humanity.

In the doctrine of the incarnation, God entered into solidarity not only with humankind but also necessarily with the whole biophysical world that humans embody and on which our existence depends. The Representative of both God and Humanity is also, therefore, the Representative of the Cosmos, the Cosmic Christ. The incarnation confers worth not only on humanity but on every life-form with which humanity is united in interdependence. Exclusively humanistic valuations seem incompatible with the incarnation. The doctrine justifies reverential care for and sparing use of our co-evolving kin.

Through the sacramental presence of the Spirit, the world is filled with the glory of God. It is the bearer of the Holy. It is valued by God as the mode of spiritual presence and residence, God's beloved habitat, and should be cherished as such by humans.

Finally, the hope for cosmic redemption—rooted in scripture (Isa. 11:6-9; 65:17, 25; Col. 1:14-20; 1 Cor. 15:28; Eph. 1:10; Rom. 8:19-22) and the main traditions of the first three or four Christian centuries—gives ultimate meaning and worth to both human and nonhuman life. This hope for a shared destiny is the ultimate confirmation of God's respect for the intrinsic value of all life. If all life will participate in God's New Creation, then all life must be treated with respect in accord with divine valuations, as ends in themselves, not simply means to human ends.

Thus, Christian understandings of God as Creator, Spirit, and Redeemer seem to imply that divine valuations are not only anthropic but also biotic, each appropriate to its kind. Respect for biotic interests, therefore, is theocentric respect for the biotic values of God.

Contrary to Derr, the fact that the command to love our neighbors is not applied specifically to nonhumans in the biblical texts does not prevent such extensions. That is an unwarranted constriction on the moral character of God. There is no inherent reason why biblical norms cannot be extended to relationships between humanity and other biota. But there are very good reasons why this extension is justified and even necessary—notably the affirmation that God is unbounded love. Thus, the logic of love encourages and even demands universal extensions. The really serious ethical problem, however, is how to express this love as a means of moral constraint in a predatorial biosphere, in which we must kill nonhuman creatures and destroy their habitats in order to survive and exercise our cultural creativity—in other words, how to become *altruistic predators.*

Intrinsic Value

Derr is right in attacking the concept of the intrinsic value of nonhuman life, for that concept is not only the foundation of his nemesis, biotic rights, but also the central threat to his anthropocentrism. Unless entities have a value for themselves, rather than merely some instrumental value for others, there is no basis for moral claims to treatment appropriate to their value. But Derr is wrong, I believe, in his interpretation of intrinsic value.

Derr ignores what I have argued is the one fundamental attribute that is necessary for recognizing intrinsic value and biotic rights: *conation.* Rights cannot be assigned arbitrarily; they must have some reasonable basis. However, the basis of biotic rights need not be the same—indeed, cannot be the same—as the grounding of human rights in universal human equality. There can be more than one basis for moral rights. One need only establish a moral status that is sufficient to warrant appropriate moral treatment from the human community. I find that basis or status in *conation*—that is, a striving to be and do, characterized by aims *or* drives, goals *or* urges, purposes *or* impulses, whether conscious *or* nonconscious, sentient *or* nonsentient. Sharing this attribute, the planet's biota, from unicellular to complex organisms, plants and animals, individuals and species, cannot be reduced to mechanized matter; they are vital and evolving forces that struggle to fulfill their reasons for being. Whatever benefits or harm they produce for others, they are good for themselves, ends in themselves, intrinsic values.

Derr is certainly right, as value theories assume: there cannot be a value without a valuer. He is mistaken, however, in assuming that humans alone supply the value—an exclusively instrumental value—to the rest of nature. He misses the point of the intrinsic value of nonhuman life: *the valuer is the nonhuman lifeform itself for itself!* Whether or not humans should honor these intrinsic values is another question, an extrinsic value judgment, but one that I have argued should be answered affirmatively on theological and philosophical grounds.

Of course, these assertions may be "immodest" or "impudent," as Derr mysteriously claims Christian biocentrists are in inferring God's purposes with the rest of nature from Christian affirmations. But if so, this inference is surely no more "immodest" or "impudent" than "insisting," as Derr does, that God's purposes are strictly anthropocentric. Seemingly, moreover, this inference is more fully compatible than Derr's with central Christian affirmations, as well as with the ecological and evolutionary reality that humans are parts and products of nature.

Biotic Rights

Derr has some good reasons for rejecting the concept of biotic rights, or the moral claims of nonhuman lifeforms. As this concept is usually interpreted by both advocates and adversaries in most of the popular and philosophical debates, I too reject it as ethically and ecologically distorted. Yet, while I too have criticized some animal rights theorists, I strongly disagree with Derr's disparagement of this movement. Far from being a "distraction," it has been a formidable and indispensable contributor to the debate. It represents one of the complementary poles—a concern for individual lifeforms—that must be balanced against a systemic or holistic pole for a comprehensive ecological ethic. Unfortunately, Derr muddles the debate involving these poles by conflating and confusing the two. He attributes characteristics to "ecocentrism" (stressing the value of collective connections, such as ecosystems) that should be used to describe "biocentrism" (emphasizing moral concern for individual lifeforms), and vice versa, in accord with current usage in the debate. For example, most ecophilosophers are ecocentrists, and reject the concept of biotic rights, which is understood as a feature of biocentrism. Derr fails to maintain the important distinctions that the two sides claim are fundamental in their continuing controversy.

It is not my task here to defend biotic rights; I have, in any case, done that at length elsewhere.[9] Yet, I must respond to Derr's particular criticisms of the concept.

Biotic rights are an effort to redefine responsible human relationships with the rest of the planet's beleaguered biota, and to ground these responsibilities not simply in human generosity and utility but in the moral claims inherent in their conation for appropriate treatment.

Biotic rights are certainly not the same full set of rights as human rights, nor are they equal rights with those of humans. Otherkind hold only the moral claims that are appropriate to the vital interests of their kind—such as claims to suitable habitat but obviously not to voting rights. Making human and nonhuman rights equal—biotic egalitarianism—is inherently unjust, because this ignores the morally relevant differences in value-creating and value-experiencing capacities between humans and all other species. Indeed, biotic rights are held against humans only, because only humans are moral agents capable of practicing justice or injustice. Biotic rights, moreover, are not moral absolutes: they can be overridden with a just cause, such as the satisfaction of significant human benefits or the exercise of self-defense. Biotic rights deny the exclusivity of human values and rights, but they do not diminish the fundamental importance of human values and rights. Biotic rights can coexist comfortably with a strong set of human rights.[10]

If biotic justice is warranted, however, all lifeforms, individuals and species, have *prima facie* claims to a "fair share" of the goods necessary for their well-being. Of course, defining a fair share is extremely difficult, especially when humans must destroy other lifeforms and their habitats for our well-being. Still, one conclusion seems clear: biotic justice imposes obligations on the human community to limit production and consumption in order to prevent the excessive exploitation and toxication of wildlife and wild lands. Profligate production and consumption are anthropocentric abuses of what God has designed for fair and frugal use in a universal covenant of justice.

The concept of biotic rights is complicated and still in an early stage of development. "Vague" and "ambiguous" criteria are certainly present, and I have been responsible for some of these. But vague and ambiguous criteria can in time be sharply formulated. Unspecified norms are not necessarily "unspecifiable," contrary to Derr. In fact, ethical norms are rarely specified as clearly in the long-standing traditions of social ethics as he seems to demand for ecological ethics.

Equally, I think Derr is wrong to opt for a theory that is "conceptually much simpler." Ethical theories in general are often necessarily complex. The appeal for simplification ducks the reality of contextual complexity and ambiguity. If the moral claims of nonhuman lifeforms are valid, they cannot be ignored to minimize complexity. The truth cannot be simplified for the sake of intellectual convenience. Moreover, the principle of parsimony is overrated: Interpretations, as Derr truly states, should not be multiplied beyond necessity, but they also should be multiplied to the point of necessity, and not insufficiently.

Similarly, Derr asserts, but does not argue, that the extension of moral rights to nonhuman lifeforms is a "serious category mistake." That is probably true of various popular and sentimental interpretations of these moral rights, but I doubt that he can make that case against ethically serious interpretations, including mine. This charge would seem to be true only if biotic rights are interpreted as being the same as or equal to human rights, but that is certainly not the argument of a number of defenders.

Derr wants to limit moral rights to intrahuman affairs. That seems arbitrary and excessively restrictive. His appeal is primarily to tradition or the customary use of rights-talk. But the appeal to tradition gets us nowhere unless one can first defend the validity of the tradition. In fact, the argument for biotic rights is intended as a rational break with the tradition, claiming that traditional usage is truncated.

In my continuing conversations with Derr on this question, I intend to question him about his relationship with his Springer Spaniels. Does he "love" them simply on the basis of his "realistic anthropocentrism," as instruments for his utility? Or is his benevolence perhaps rooted in their moral claims on him? Does he tacitly recognize moral obligations to them? My suspicion is that Tom's intuitive conduct is sometimes a biologically broader embrace than his theory permits. That reminds me of an exchange with a student who thought biotic rights was an odd idea. I asked if she would strangle a baby robin in the nest, assuming she was not exceptionally hungry. "Of course, not!" she replied emphatically. "Why not?" I continued. "Because it has a right to be let alone," she answered, and then added an enlightened afterthought: "Oops!"

Ecofeminism

Ecofeminism is a multinational, multidisciplinary, and multi-faith phenomenon. It is a diverse and developing movement, filled with a variety of viewpoints and internal disagreements.[11] Thus, it is truly a daring deed for Derr to analyze and critique the movement as a whole. But it is equally a doomed deed, foiled by its own audacity and simplicity.

The very title of Derr's section, "The Ecofeminist Distraction," suggests a categorical dismissal of and disdain for the ecofeminist agenda, and that perception is confirmed by the tone and substance of the section itself. My wife and daughters, from whom I sought counsel on that section, described it, rightly I believe, as "condescending," "insulting," even "paternalistic." It is not even clear what ecofeminism is a distraction from, other than Derr's "true view" on environmental matters—an attitude which in itself suggests the unworthiness of an adversary for serious debate. This section of his essay will not stimulate dialogue with feminists; it will—and should—alienate.

Derr is right, however, on one fundamental point: the core concept of ecofeminism—its unitive factor, as ecofeminists agree—is the recognition of close connections, historically and ideologically, between patriarchalism in male–female relations and anthropocentrism in ecological relations. The devaluation or subjugation of women and the rest of nature are intimately linked. Both are treated as instruments or objects for exploitation. But contrary to Derr, this interpretation of reality is hardly trivial; it points to some shared roots of sexism and ecological degradation that demand serious attention and response. Ecofeminism seems to be an appropriate combination of concerns.

The ecofeminist movement does not entail "a wholesale denigration of men"; it is not a manifestation of "sexism," as Derr charges. Anti-patriarchalism is directed against male domination and domineering values, not against men as individuals or as a gender—an important distinction that Derr misses. Instead, ecofeminism generally intends and promises healing and enhancing relationships between both men and women and humans and the rest of nature. In my experiences with ecofeminists, my perspectives have been received fairly and often favorably by the vast majority. Disagreements have been with particular persons and usually on given propositions. Thus, in this case, like Edmund Burke, I do not know how to draw up an indictment against a whole movement.

Derr's basic problem in analysis and evaluation is again the indiscriminate consolidation of contraries. He recognizes the diversity in the movement and acknowledges major exceptions to the faults he claims to find in the whole. Yet, he disregards these exceptions in constructing his criticisms of this imaginary whole. Indeed, the exceptions are often the leading lights of the movement, such as Carolyn Merchant and Rosemary Radford Ruether, as well as several other Christian ecofeminists whom Derr does not reference, such as Carol Robb, Lois K. Daly, and Sallie McFague. These women represent prominent counterfacts, indicative of Derr's faulty generalizations.

For instance, Derr argues that the idea that "women are closer to nature" is part of the essence of ecofeminism. But then he admits that not all ecofeminists accept this defining feature. Bizarre indeed is the notion that an entity can lack an attribute that defines its being! In reality, this idea, advanced by some "nature feminists," is rejected by many ecofeminists. Lois Daly even argues that this position is challenged by ecofeminism itself.[12]

Similarly, contra Derr, ecofeminists do not necessarily or even generally succumb to biotic egalitarianism. They are not necessarily or generally hostile to technology, or guilty of "Luddite anger," or

114

opposed to "third world development." They do not subscribe to a "prescientific worldview" or romanticize tribal cultures. These are characteristics of particular, perhaps many, individuals, but they are not attributes of a movement or even most individuals in that movement. Ecofeminism has no single or specific theology. It embodies both Christian and multiple non-Christian manifestations, which Derr recognizes but strangely scrambles in his assessments. It is guilt by association, for example, to berate Christian ecofeminists for the rejection of "Western monotheism" or the acceptance of neopaganism by some of their non-Christian peers.

Finally, contrary to Derr, ecofeminism is anything but anti-humanistic. The very fact that it is a form of feminism indicates the prominence of concern for inclusive human rights and humane relationships. In fact, one criticism that can be made of some ecofeminists is that the human agenda is so dominant in their projects that ecological relationships are reduced to a secondary status or even a formality. That is not a complaint, however, that the anthropocentric Derr can make.

Derr has created a "strawwoman"—an imaginary monolith, a stationary target set up for easy hits. In reality, however, the only way ecofeminism can be dismissed as a distraction is if its central contention—the invidious linkage between patriarchalism and anthropocentric exclusivism—can be refuted. Derr rejects it, even ridicules it, but he really makes no effort to refute it. Yet, if that contention is defensible, as I believe it is, then ecofeminism is anything but a distraction; it offers a profound revelation on the human condition.

Environmental Policies

Derr's analysis of various environmental issues is not simply an expression of the "cool-headed reason" to which he aspires. It is also, to some degree, a reflection of a prominent political ideology. Despite the occasional guise of showing "both sides," Derr shows a preference for the positions of the environmental critics on the political Right, for whom the Great Green Specter has replaced the Red Scare as the obsession of choice. Against environmentalists, who are routinely dismissed as "alarmists," Derr favorably cites such conservative stalwarts as Julian Simon, Charles Rubin, Peter J. Hill, and Ronald Bailey. In discussing climate change, his points show the clear influence of Patrick J. Michaels, a politically conservative climatologist and well-known panner of the global warming theory.[13] Resorting to innuendo, Derr hints that many environmentalists are really "reds" or even "green totalitarians."

Yet, the influence of the political Right on Derr is not so strong that he succumbs to the private property panaceas and antigovernment libertarianism of the Free Marketeers. He rejects these solutions, and recognizes the need for a balance between individual freedom and the common good. Though market mechanisms are his preferred form of public regulation, he does not advocate deregulation. In fact, he says that governmental regulations are a major reason for environmental improvements in the United States. I suspect that in general Derr would agree with me: in an age when the denigration of government has become routinized, it is important to stress that our human rights demand not only protections *from* the tyrannies of government, but also protections *by* government *against* the tyrannies of privateers. Derr's overall political philosophy shows considerable eclectic breeding, with evident effects from various forms of conservatism and progressivism. He is probably near the center on the American political spectrum. Nonetheless, Derr's views on environmental issues show clear signs of substantial shaping by the political Right.

Following this lead, Derr accuses the environmental movement—transformed now into a monolithic ideology called "apocalyptic environmental*ism*"—of a "legacy of false alarms." Allegedly, environmentalists have exaggerated their case in order to encourage terrified conversions to the environmental cause, and have distracted attention from more important concerns (though what these are is unclear). No doubt, one can find plenty of examples of inflations of fact, but this problem is not a peculiar feature of the environmental movement. In fact, Derr himself and the political Right greatly exaggerate the sins of their opponents. Moreover, Derr completely ignores the far more common and impressive legacy of *true* alarms, from such diverse voices as Rachel Carson, Aldo Leopold, E. O. Wilson, and, one of Derr's favorite targets, Paul Ehrlich.

Like the environmental skeptics on the political Right, Derr doubts the severity of most environmental problems. His frequent understatement of problems lends a credence to complacency. On human-induced climate change and ozone depletion, he says that the cases for these alleged dangers are not sufficiently compelling to justify the great expenses of economic conversion, and, if necessary, we can adapt technologically. On diverse forms of pollution, our society still has a long way to go to solutions, but the situation is improving, and we must, in any case, reject the quest for "zero tolerance"—another straw target, since the vast majority of environmentalists understands the dilemmas of marginal impacts. Derr denies the dangers of insufficient food production, as prophesied by those he describes as "doomsayers" and "Luddites." Biotechnology can enable us to overcome global hunger. Similarly, on the dangers of resource exhaustion, Derr trusts in market pricing to save us.

Regarding the extinctions of species and the serious reductions in their populations, Derr seems concerned but hardly alarmed. He repeats the now-traditional but still tacky *ad hominem* that environmentalists are more concerned about the perils of penguins than the plight of the poor. He also joins in the dismissal of the Right's latest nemesis, the Endangered Species Act, which he says is of "doubtful value" in protecting species—a claim that bypasses the evidence for the act's significant achievements despite a limited mandate and resources.[14] Moreover, he casually commends cost-benefit analysis, apparently oblivious to the moral opposition to economic types of this method that reduce moral values to subjective, market preferences,[15] and to the political Right's advocacy of this method in the Congress as a way to stifle effective environmental regulation.

Derr commendably appeals for a synthesis of environmental quality and economic development for poor nations, including as a means to resolve the population problem. He neglects to mention, however, that this goal has become a main plank in the platform of the mainstream environmental movement—including the 1992 United Nations Conference on Environment and Development at Rio,[16] the significance of which Derr dismisses. From the perspective of many contemporary environmentalists, economic deprivation is a major cause and effect of ecological degradation in a vicious cycle that destroys resources and further propels poverty. Thus, economic justice is not only an essential good in itself but also an essential condition of ecological integrity—and vice versa.

Derr's position on population growth is unclear. He largely ignores the critical social and ecological problems that will arise from adding nearly one billion people per decade and nearly doubling the world's human population from the already harmfully high figure of 5.7 billion in 1996 to more than 10 billion in 2050. He saves his wrath for the "elitist" controllers of population.

Only one area of environmental concern arouses Derr's alarm: the loss of farmlands and forests, primarily as a consequence of "rapacious economic interests." He is a "countryman" who "loves" the land. I commend his passionate commitment on this concern. I wish, however, that he would generalize from this experience, recognizing that every dimension of the ecological crisis is a real threat to "the land," and "the land" that deserves to be loved, as Aldo Leopold taught us, is not only the farms and forests but the whole bountiful biosphere and all its inhabitants.

Derr has considerable confidence in the free market and technology to prevent resource shortages for the future. That confidence, however, appears to me excessive, and as such, productive of hallucinatory hopes. It fosters the illusion that nature's capacities are practically inexhaustible, and encourages economic strategies for living beyond planetary means. The ecological reality, however, is that the earth has biophysical limits, and even with human technological powers to improve output, we now seem to be approaching or surpassing some of those limits, locally and/or globally, in both renewable and nonrenewable resources, as well as in wastes produced.

Look, for example, at nonrenewable resources—which include fossil fuels and minerals such as iron and bauxite. They are used in massive amounts under the prods of population and consumption growth. By definition, nonrenewables will run out—or become too cost-ineffective to extract (which is functionally the same). The implicit question in much of the debate has been whether practical exhaustion will be in the short- or long-run. That question does not make an ethical difference, however, if we have equitable responsibilities to future generations. At present, the resource base of industrially significant metals is certainly adequate for the short-term, measured myopically in decades. Plus, new discoveries occur regularly, and new technologies now make extractions from some known deposits cost-effective. At current production levels of economically extractable reserves, these metals will last from 18 years in the case of lead to 222 years in the case of aluminum.[17] The actual productive years will probably be considerably longer with new discoveries. Yet, if significant growth continues in the consumption of these minerals, as it almost certainly will, market-based shortages and increased costs may occur sooner rather than later.

Contrary to environmental optimists like Derr, the market is not an adequate indicator of long-term environmental scarcity—the

118

natural, yet-untapped resource base. Market prices reflect available supply and demand in a commodity at a particular or projected time, rising or falling with shortages or surpluses. They are not reliable indicators of long-term future shortages. There is an important difference between market scarcity and environmental scarcity, which is usually unrecognized in the debates about the dangers of emerging resource exhaustion. Current market prices tell us little about a rapidly declining resource, until that point in the future when market scarcity and environmental scarcity begin to converge. Until that point, it is possible to have an increasing supply and declining prices in the market. By that point, however, it is largely too late to conserve a commodity for the sake of future generations.

Yet, technology, as Derr notes, can help us to extend the limits of nonrenewable resources. Recycling is now widespread. Substitution of one mineral for another is technologically possible in some cases—like fiber optics for copper (the example most commonly cited, almost as if this instance can be universalized). Renewables can sometimes be substituted for nonrenewables. But substitutions are not guaranteed; technology is not alchemy. And even when substitutes are technically feasible, what eventually will substitute for the substitutes? What will replace the petrochemical plastics that now often replace metals? While technological improvements are truly impressive and will be indispensable for the human future, it is well to remember that technology, too, is subject to biophysical limits. And it cannot restore extinct species or most simplified ecosystems. On nonrenewable resources (as well as renewables—like fisheries, forests, and soils, which can become functionally nonrewable when pushed beyond their bounds of tolerance), there really are no moral substitutes for careful conservation, comprehensive recycling, ultraefficiency, constrained consumption, and product durability and repairability.

Another major issue that Derr raises is: will food supplies be adequate for the impending future, or will they be overwhelmed by human numbers? Despite some optimistic predictions, predicated on high confidence in genetic technology and a naive expectation of human prudence, the answer to this question remains uncertain. Some signs appear ominous. To meet anticipated demands from population growth, the nations will need at least a doubling of food production by the middle of the next century.[18] But fish harvests, a prime source of animal protein in many low-income countries, are

119

declining globally. Overfishing has dangerously depleted stocks of most commercial fisheries worldwide—including the once bounteous cod off the coasts of New England and the Canadian maritime provinces, where the main fishing banks are now closed. The world catch has been declining since the peak year of 1989 (about 100 million tons), after a nearly five-fold increase since 1950.[19] Moreover, grain production increases have been slowing, dropping below the rate of population growth and thereby reducing per capita availability.[20] Active strategies for reducing population growth seem imperative for meeting the food challenge.

Derr also highlights the problem of moral decision-making under conditions of uncertainty, particularly the difficulty for the layperson of weighing "conflicting appraisals" by the "experts." The problem is real, but it is not restricted to amateurs. Scientific professionals, studying everything from the ecological effects of pesticides to forestry practices, often express concern about the great degree of uncertainty in risk analyses. Data are generally incomplete, often inconclusive, and, of course, disputable. Tools are imperfect and methods depend on debatable assumptions. Causation is often difficult or even impossible to establish firmly; inferences of various levels of probability may be the only options.

Thus, Derr's point is sound. But that point does not ordinarily justify the "moderation" that he recommends, let alone the denial of the magnitude of environmental risks that his discussion exudes. On the contrary, in the context of high risk, where the consequences of scientific miscalculation can be severe or even catastrophic, reasonable fears and suspicions may justify precisely the decisive warnings and actions that Derr dismisses as alarmism. Climate change provides a useful illustration of these contrasting approaches to high-risk decision-making.

Human-induced climate change might not happen, and if it does, the consequences might be more or less than feared. Maybe the climatologists have failed to consider all the variables and their interactions. Thus, one might argue that the nations should, in the absence of conclusive evidence, maintain the status quo and avoid environmental policies that might disrupt economic stability. Yet, most atmospheric scientists, worldwide, warn that climate change and some dire attendant effects are highly probable. Should we simply ignore their reasoned predictions and fears until they can provide conclusive evidence—which is virtually impossible? What if it is then too late, as the specialists worry, to take remedial action? What are the potential effects of following the moral counsel of the complacent, as Derr prefers, against the potential effects of following the moral counsel of the reasonably fearful?

The worst moral response to the threat of global warming, or any other severe risk, is an indecisive, business-as-usual policy. That approach courts danger. Waiting for surety in this setting is avoiding a remedy.

In contrast, the best moral response to such threats seems to be a "preferential option" for social and ecological security. In situations of uncertainty where there are some reasonable grounds for fear of adverse outcomes, it is morally appropriate to act decisively to prevent or minimize a potential social or ecological harm, even at the risk of being wrong. This approach shifts the burden of proof in favor of health and environmental interests. On climate change, it means taking the steps necessary to reduce its effects and doing so quickly.

This low-risk strategy is morally preferable to Derr's response in both the best-case and worst-case scenarios. On the one hand, if the fears about global warming are exaggerations, the nations will still gain major social and ecological benefits, because every tactic to combat global warming can be justified as essential on other grounds. With or without climate change, we will still benefit from ecologically safe and renewable alternatives to fossil fuels, an efficiency revolution, reforestation, and the elimination of chlorofluorocarbons. Either way, we will still need an economic conversion to ecological sustainability and social equity in the distribution of finite resources. On the other hand, if global warming is no exaggeration, the nations may avoid catastrophe by acting decisively now. This strategy is true caution and sensible insurance. Interestingly, this strategy is now being pushed by some major international actors in the insurance and banking industries, driven by "the brute strength of the marketplace" to protect their financial interests from weather-created disasters.[21]

In the midst of scientific and moral uncertainty, Derr would do well to consider an alternative approach to high risk. He might then perceive some so-called alarmism as a reasonable alert and a plausible ground for decisive action against an alarming situation.

Social Consequences of Biocentrism

Derr describes some of the social consequences of biotic values and rights with some accuracy—for example, the protection of species for their sake as well as ours, the burden of proof on human interventions in wild ecosystems, and economic frugality. But he often leaves out important qualifications. And he indiscriminately lumps the reasonable and the eccentric together in one place—maintaining that biotic values imply the abandonment of zoos, flower gardens, animal experiments, pets, recreational hunting, Halloween pumpkins, Christmas trees, "monuments in the wild" (like Mount Rushmore), the suppression of forest fires, and the benevolent rescue of injured wild creatures. Probably all of these ideas have surfaced among a few proponents, but none—except killing animals for fun or glory, in my opinion—can be described as a normal and necessary consequence of biotic values. Yet, a few of these ideas have been defended by serious thinkers offering substantive arguments. For example, a good case can be made for allowing "free burns" of lightning-induced forest fires in some wild areas as a natural part of ecological cycles. Derr, however, gives no hint of these arguments. (Incidentally, I hope there are no more Mount Rushmores; the case against the one can be argued on strictly aesthetic grounds!)

Subsequently, Tom moves beyond oversimplifications and caricatures to serious accusations. These are directed initially at the "extremes" but quickly generalized to cover the whole of biocentrism and its allies, including ecofeminism and the animal rights movement. Biocentrism, he says, is inherently fatalistic; it cultivates "indifference to the human prospect." Human extinction is of no moral significance. On the question of whether nature should be allowed to take its course in human affairs, and, thus, whether humans should curtail the use of medicines and refrain from feeding the hungry in order "to apply this ecological wisdom," he claims that "the whole direction of biocentric thought" is to answer this question affirmatively. These are the "social implications of their theory."

These are weighty charges. No doubt, a very small percentage of extreme or pure biocentrists—or far more likely, extreme ecocentrists, such as some deep ecologists—can be justly so accused. But the charges are indefensible against the vast majority of those whose thought embodies biocentric and/or ecocentric elements. Again, Derr's collective critique causes trouble: he combines a variety of disparate ethical views into an artificial and unwarranted whole, and then criticizes this whole for the flawed perspectives of some of the parts—flaws that many who represent parts of this imagined whole would reject as strongly as Derr does. It is no wonder most biocentrists "recoil" from the alleged "social implications of their theory." The reason is that there are no such implications! They simply do not follow, not inductively nor deductively.

For most of us who have described our thought as biocentric or as having biocentric elements, we have tried, in different ways and with different results, to integrate anthropic, biotic, and ecosystemic values into our social and ecological ethics, without jeopardizing our commitment to the human project. In fact, we believe that a commitment to biotic and ecosystemic values enhances the human prospect by preventing the excessive and imprudent destruction of the human habitat. Those of us who are Christians believe with Derr that God cares deeply about the human prospects on this planet; but it does not follow logically that God cares *exclusively* about human prospects or that biotic values cannot be integrated with human values.

Nevertheless, Derr's essay offers an important warning to those of us who have used the word "biocentric," perhaps loosely, to describe our ethical perspectives. If the word, particularly the suffix, connotes to some, as it apparently does to Derr, that the "life process as a whole" is "the primary locus of value," without moral distinctions among lifeforms and between humans and all other lifeforms, then we need to find a better word to communicate our intentions effectively. That connotation is clearly not what most of us intend. Our intention is not to substitute biotic values for anthropic ones, but rather to supplement the latter with the former and to weave them together coherently for the enhancement of both. This integration of anthropic and biotic values, of social justice and ecological justice— a union that is often called "ecojustice" in some Christian circles[22]— is a critical task for both ethics and public policy in our age.

Conclusion

The environmental movement is dramatically diverse, filled with numerous divisions and interests. As a whole and in its many parts, it displays the range of wisdom and folly, the good and bad, to which all human flesh is heir. It has immense strengths and weaknesses.

Yet, the movement is too valuable to be bashed or abandoned. It merits constant correction and nurture. Indeed, the environmental movement must be empowered to become a match for the environmental cause—confronting effectively that conglomerate of social and ecological problems that imperil human and biospheric well-being. This environmental cause requires creative reforms of the truncated values and policies that prevail in our nation and the community of nations. It challenges us to follow a new course—a course that lives within the bounds of nature's regenerative, absorptive, and carrying capacities; one that adapts prudently to the interdependence of humans with all other planetary elements and processes; and one that responds benevolently and justly to the fact of human kinship with all otherkind.

Chapter 3

Christ and Creation's Longing

Richard John Neuhaus

In 1971, I published *In Defense of People*,[1] the first book-length critique of the "ecology movement" that was then in ascendancy and that pretty much shaped the arguments that continue to swirl around varieties of environmentalism today. There are significant differences between then and now. Then there was a thing called "the movement" (often capitalized as The Movement), which was a frequently confused mix of agitations coming out of the civil rights movement, joining up with opposition to the war in Vietnam, and linking hands with a "counterculture" that embraced everything from pharmaceutical ecstasies to flirting with revolutionary violence. The movement with which I was identified had to do with racial justice and peace. I and others of like mind criticized the drug culture and related antics as a self-indulgent distraction from the goals of racial justice and peace, and worried that the new enthusiasm for "ecological consciousness" was in fact a conservative ploy designed to turn the movement away from the cause of the poor.

Put differently, by the end of the 1960s environmentalism was applying for full membership in the movement. Although there was no tidy definition of the movement's leadership, it was understood that the movement had the power to certify what was legitimately liberal—remembering that in those tumultuous days liberalism routinely called itself radical. *In Defense of People* was my argument that the ecology movement, if admitted at all, should be admitted on probation. I pointed out, among other things, that environmentalism had historically been an aristocratic and decidedly conservative cause. It had unsavory associations with anti-immigration and even eugenic enthusiasms, and betrayed a distinct distaste for common people whom, as Lincoln observed, God must love since he made so many of them. Hence the title of the book, *In Defense of People*.

I recall that at the time my editor at Macmillan worried that the book might be making too much of the phenomenon, that all the talk about ecology was "a flash in the pan." Reviewers in *The New York Times* and elsewhere opined that ecology was little more than a commonsensical concern for global housekeeping, and quite innocent of the far-reaching and rather alarming implications about which I warned. That, of course, was before the full-blown philosophies of "deep ecology" and "radical environmentalism" so lucidly analyzed by Thomas Derr. Suffice it that my argument did not carry the day, and environmentalism was admitted to full membership in the movement as an integral part of that cause of all causes, Social Change. Also in circles such as the World Council of Churches, environmentalism was patched on to the quilt of peace and justice, and presented as a seamless garment of progressive commitment. Derr's account nicely depicts the uncritical ease with which this fusion was effected.

The gravamen of *In Defense of People* is summarized in Derr's succinct paragraph:

> Beyond their misunderstanding of the facts, beyond their tolerance of draconian solutions, the [environmental and population] controllers are finally accused of regarding people, at least when found in great numbers, as a kind of pollution. There is among them that dreadful elitist assumption of the wealthy and comfortable that lesser lives are not worth living. There is more than a touch of "first world" imperialism here, and it may explain why environmentalists are more excited about habitat and species protection than about human health in the poor nations: the human species is not endangered, and could use a little thinning out.[2]

In the twenty-five years since the publication of *In Defense of People*, I have tried to follow the development of the arguments, but not with the indefatigable energy and assiduous care exemplified by Thomas Derr. He has shown an almost heroic patience in attending to the pertinent literature, and responding to arguments point by point. It takes great patience because in fact the arguments have not substantively developed all that much. There is regular change of rhetoric, and the tocsin of environmental alarmism is sounded in different keys and with reference to different scientific (or pseudo-scientific) claims, but the shape of the argument has not changed that much in the past quarter century. It was all there, at least in nascent form, in 1971 and, in fact, much earlier.

Readers who have not been paying close attention to these controversies may think that Derr's essay is at times excessively harsh or unfair. On the contrary, he is not only patient, he is charitable almost to a fault. How should one respond to writers such as Paul Ehrlich, whose stock in trade is reckless hyperbole and outright prevarication? What attitude should we take to Garrett Hardin, who claims to be intellectually and morally courageous in urging that we brace ourselves for the deliberate elimination of millions of expendable human beings? I fear it is a mark of the corruption of our intellectual and academic discourse that it is deemed necessary to respond to such people as though they are making arguments that intelligent and decent people must take seriously. In a saner world we would be less hesitant to say that some people are inveterate liars and moral barbarians, denizens of fever swamps far removed from the civilized world for which we are responsible. Regrettably, however, the fever swamps press in upon us, and we must attend to the dikes if the possibility of a human and humane world is to be preserved.

Thomas Derr renders a great service in attending to the intellectual and moral dikes, in alerting us to the incoherences, dishonesties, and very real dangers of philosophical and practical proposals being advanced in the name of environmentalism. The fair-minded reader will recognize that he does all this within the framework of a profound, informed, and religiously grounded concern for the integrity of creation. In responding to Derr's important essay, I want to extend the argument to consider sympathetically some urgent truths that are being badly mangled in the confused agitations of radical environmentalism or, as it is called, deep ecology. I will not address the specific policy disputes that Derr handles with admirable sobriety, but will instead attend to some of the philosophical and theological questions that inform, and deform, current debates.

I am more uneasy than Derr seems to be with the term "anthropocentric." Against those who hold humanity in contempt, I, too, want to declare myself a humanist and join in the most elevated and elevating tradition of a culture that celebrates man as "the crown of creation." That humanism is a great and fragile achievement, the result of a long, bloody, and tortuous process that reaches from the slaughter of virgins in appeasement of vengeful gods to the abolition of slavery to the recognition of Auschwitz and the Gulag Archipelago as icons of the evil of which we are capable. Upon the historical achievements of this humanism depends the sustainability of a liberal democratic social order and the philosophy of human rights that undergirds that order. But I do not think we should call this humanism "anthropocentric."

Better we should speak of a theocentric perspective or, better yet, a theonomous perspective. The "theos" in question need not, at least in the first instance, speak of the One whom Christians call God. It does speak of that which transcends the human, of that which, to put it more cautiously, is not exhausted by the human. There is a correct intuition that wants to "situate" humanity within something greater than humanity. Man is not the only thing in the universe, and is not the greatest thing in the universe. Some of those whom Derr criticizes are right about that. Humanity's dignity and grandeur are derived. The religious impulse, evident also in radical environmentalism, rightly recoils from making an idol of humanity. The "theos" points to the "other" from which human dignity and grandeur (and responsibility!) are derived.

In refusing to make an idol of humanity, some species of environmental thought make an idol of the universe itself. Nature becomes the theos, the other, the god (or, more frequently, the goddess.) This is the result of a legitimate religious impulse gone astray. James Gustafson, whom Derr discusses, keeps that impulse within a tighter discipline by his accent on the theocentric as distinct from the anthropocentric. Although the argument needs much more development than I can give it here, I would suggest that Gustafson's approach is insufficiently *Christ*-ian. Classical Christianity provides a more adequate way of "situating" humanity by reference to the God-Man, Jesus Christ. Theocentrism and anthropocentrism give way to Christology, the understanding that Jesus Christ is both true God and true man. In this Christocentric view, humanity is fully participant in an order best described as theonomous, a reality ordered by God and to God.

Nor is nature in any way left out of this theonomous order as it is Christocentrically constructed. I would emphasize more strongly than does Derr the New Testament passages found in Romans, Ephesians, Revelation, and elsewhere that underscore the "cosmic Christ." It is not simply Eastern Orthodoxy but the legacy of all Christians that lifts up the promise of the "deification" of all things.

In the letter to the Colossians, for instance, St. Paul dramatically situates God, man, and nature in Christ:

> He is the image of the invisible God, the first-born of all creation; for in him all things were created, in heaven and on earth, visible and invisible, whether thrones or dominions or principalities or authorities—all things were created through him and for him. He is before all things, and in him all things hold together. He is the head of the body, the church; he is the beginning, the first-born from the dead, that in everything he might be preeminent. For in him all the fullness of God was pleased to dwell, and through him to reconcile to himself all things, whether on earth or in heaven, making peace by the blood of his cross. (Col. 1:15-20, RSV)

Derr effectively challenges those polemicists who blame the Judeo-Christian tradition for our environmental problems because it allegedly teaches an idea of "dominion" that excuses unlimited exploitation of our natural habitat. As he says, the ideas of stewardship and delegated dominion impose very real limits on what we can do. But those ideas, as important as they are, do not adequately "situate" man environmentally; they fail to convey the full force of our participation in the destiny of all things. One of the problems, I suspect, is that contemporary Christians do not take as seriously as we should our human embodiment and our hope for the resurrection of the body. Although she is not specifically addressing environmental thought, this is an argument pressed by Caroline Walker Bynum in her recent and remarkable study, *The Resurrection of the Body in Western Christianity*.[3]

Among both Protestants and Catholics today, there is a growing literature on the theology of the body. The vision proposed, a vision that radically situates humanity in the drama of creation, is addressed by Dominican theologian Benedict Ashley:

> Thus in the physical universe, to the infinite creativity of God corresponds the infinite potentiality of matter. And in that ocean of matter, in the ever shifting and transient forms that cross it, we can see the face of God reflected, in what the medievals called the Mirror of God. Yet that metaphor of the mirror is too Platonic, because God's epiphany in the world is not through mere surface shadows, but is in the coming to be, development, and passing away to make room for novelty of primary natural units, each of which truly exists and acts in its own right and according to its own nature and structure for its time, and interacts with other units in a process of mutual actualization and eventual replacement. The

physical universe is not a mere shadow, it is a drama of billions of actors, some minute, blindly moving atoms, some living plants and moving animals, and some intelligent body-persons enacting an evolutionary history whose scenario still remains open to the future.[4]

The avenues of thought explored by Ashley and others are reminiscent of the earlier work of the Jesuit theologian and scientist Teilhard de Chardin. Teilhard, of course, was suspected by some of deviating from Christian orthodoxy, and his notion of the "hominization" of the universe has been interpreted—unfairly, I think—as a truly relentless form of anthroprocentrism. His accent, rather, was on the "Christification" of all things along the lines suggested by the passage from Colossians cited above. In any event, it seems to me more than probable that the promptings of environmental thought, combined with intensified interaction between science and theology, will in the years ahead produce an efflorescence of Christian reflection that unfolds as yet undeveloped truths that are latent in cardinal doctrines such as creation, redemption, and the promise of bodily resurrection.

At several points Derr contrasts Christian and "secular" accounts of the relationship between humanity and nature. I believe he is closer to the promising and problematic heart of the matter when he recognizes that these other accounts are not really secular but are religious or quasi-religious in character. Like what we usually call religion, they attempt to provide a "meaning system" or an "explanation of everything." As Derr notes, for some people environmental philosophies, and even environmental spiritualities, are a replacement for Marxist and other meaning systems that no longer seem plausible. Thus the recoloration of ideologies from "red" to "green." But I expect that some forms of "deep ecology" do indeed go deeper than that. They are intuitive and frequently confused probings toward a comprehensive construction of reality. Call it a construction of reality, a narrative, a myth, or whatever—it is a movement of sensibilities and ideas that gropes toward an encompassing account that tries to make sense—not least of all moral sense—of human culture that is neither lost in the cosmos nor at war with it.

These questions are not new to Christian thought, but today they press with renewed urgency. There is a formidable Christian intellectual tradition addressing these questions; it includes, inter alia, figures so estimable as Origin, Irenaeus, Thomas Aquinas, Teilhard, and, in our own day, thinkers such as Wolfhart Pannenberg. In view of this impressive intellectual tradition, it seems odd that so many environmental thinkers (some of whom call themselves eco-philosophers or eco-theologians) seem to think that they are starting from scratch, sniffing about in the ruins of god and goddess myths, piecing together the venerated shards of primitive worldviews, or frankly inventing new world-stories such as sundry versions of the Gaia hypothesis.

On second thought, however, it is not so completely odd that people think they are starting from scratch. We can hardly overestimate the consequences of the fact that most intellectuals today are religiously illiterate, and are most particularly innocent of any knowledge of the Christian intellectual tradition. They may say that modern (or postmodern) thought has "moved beyond" what Aquinas, for instance, had to say about the interaction of nature and history, but in fact they typically have not the foggiest notion of what Aquinas said, or even whether he said anything at all on the subject. Like Thomas Derr, I have a fondness for Occam's razor, and one should not look for additional explanations of the foolish things people write when ignorance suffices. Of course there are exceptions, but the instances of religious and quasi-religious inventiveness cited by Derr (which are all too easy to parody) generally represent excitements untempered by education.

An inquiry into the causes of this widespread illiteracy would require an extended discussion of the state of what we persist in calling higher education. But there are several factors that can be noted briefly. The phrase "Christian intellectual tradition" is thought by many to be oxymoronic since they have been led to believe (frequently with the encouragement of misguided Christians) that Christianity has to do with faith while the intellectual life has to do with reason, and these are two different ways of speaking about reality that cannot speak to one another. In addition, in our current academic ambiance it is widely established as a matter of dogma that "Western culture" is the source of the ills that plague humanity and planet earth. In environmental circles, as Derr notes, that dogma is powerfully reinforced by the conventional polemic against the biblical language of domination. Never mind that the Christian intellectual tradition is more than "Western" in the usual use of the term, and never mind that there is nothing more uniquely Western than the pattern of self-criticism that easily turns into self-hatred, it is true that Christianity is undeniably and foundationally entangled with the West, and that is enough, in the minds of many intellectuals, to put it beyond the pale.

Nor, because it is so obvious, should we underestimate a more personal factor. The writers discussed by Derr, plus many others he might have cited, typically come out of a Christian background. "Come out of" and "background"—the terms are telling. Christianity is something in their past, something they have outgrown; no doubt many would say something that they have escaped. That is the past: "Been there, done that." Ideas must be new, they must be about change, about the future. In the realm of ideas, the myth of linear progress has an unbreakable hold also on the minds of conservationists who understand themselves to be at war with the myth of progress. To seriously entertain the possibility that the Christian tradition may hold some of the answers for which they are looking would be to go backward, even though for most of these writers it would be going back to where they had never been except as children with a Sunday School impression of Christian doctrine.

Moreover, for a certain kind of writer on the left ideas must bear a revolutionary panache, and there is a frisson of defiance in taking one's stance with, say, the Druids of old (reinvented and sanitized, to be sure, without, for instance, the burning of human sacrifices). This intellectual posture of fancied defiance is tiresomely familiar in our intellectual history. As someone has remarked, everything changes except the avant garde. Even the most eccentric reconstruction of presumably primitive myths can provide the avant garde with a place to stand in opposition to Christianity and Western culture, which are declared to be both thoroughly discredited and powerfully holding humanity in thrall.

And so there are many reasons why Christian wisdom has a hard time gaining a hearing among environmental thinkers who are in search of a religious or quasi-religious construal of reality that can comprehend their concerns. A change in this circumstance will require that, in the years and decades ahead, orthodox Christian thinkers demonstrate that Christianity provides a more plausible and promising account of the legitimate concerns raised by environmentalists. As with thinkers such as Teilhard, such efforts will have to, as they say, press the envelope, and they will sometimes be viewed as theologically suspect. As in any serious intellectual venture, there are risks of taking wrong turns. Such exploration should be undertaken within a community and tradition that provide necessary correctives by reference to the rule of faith (*regula fidei*) and teaching authority (*magisterium*).

The exploration must be undertaken, however. I have already mentioned some of the Christian thinkers who are engaging these questions, but much more needs to be done. It is too easy for orthodox Christians to parody and dismiss the more sensationalist popularizers of "creation theology" such as Rosemary Ruether, Matthew Fox, and Thomas Berry. The sometimes bizarre manner of their expression should not blind us to the legitimate concerns being raised. The fact is that Western Christianity, especially in the post-Reformation period, has been preoccupied with the question of individual salvation. That is, of course, a question of surpassing urgency for each of us. But the preoccupation with that question has contributed to a failure to do justice to the cosmic dimensions of the Christian message. Too many philosophers and religious thinkers, including serious Christians, have thought it necessary to look outside the Christian tradition for a way of understanding the nature and destiny of the universe, when a more convincing account can be developed from within the tradition. Such a development will require a fuller engagement with Eastern Orthodox theology, and with the rich and oft-neglected resources of the early Christian centuries as these are available to us in the patristic literature.

It is observed that every heresy is a truth that has lost its balance, and at present, as well as in the past, flirtation with heresy and heresy itself have attended much thinking about the relationship between God and his creation. There is, for example, the perennial temptation to pantheism. In the same breath that orthodox writers condemn pantheism, they frequently condemn panentheism as well. I would suggest—with, I hope, appropriate caution—that some distinctions are in order here. Pantheism is clearly incompatible with the Great Tradition of Christian thought. Pantheism is the claim that God is all there is or that all is God. It is a radical immanentism that denies the transcendence of God. Although there is some dispute about his teaching, it would seem that Spinoza, for example, equated God with the systematic perfection of the world order. In pantheism, God engulfs all, which theoretically results in negating what is not God. The practical result, somewhat paradoxically, is the negation of God as an unnecessary hypothesis. When all is God, there is no need for God.

Panentheism is crucially different. *Pan-en-theos* literally means everything in God. The coining of the term is usually attributed to the German philosopher Karl C. F. Krause (1781–1832), who wanted to articulate more clearly the position of Kant. In that idealistic tradition, but giving it a more mystical turn, Krause posited God as the primordial being that contains the universe but is apart from it and superior to it, with human consciousness being a participation in the mind of God toward which nature is evolving. Quite apart from Krause's enterprise, one finds elements of panentheism in Plato's being and becoming, in Nicholas of Cusa's Infinite that reconciles all opposites, in the Absolute Spirit of Hegel, in Whitehead's process theology, and in Teilhard's understanding of creation evolving toward the Omega Point. Hans Urs von Balthasar has insightfully traced the ways in which the identification of God, creation, and human consciousness strongly shaped both the theistic and atheistic streams of eighteenth- and nineteenth-century Romanticism.[5] The second volume of Wolfhart Pannenberg's *Systematic Theology* is a particularly rich resource for understanding contemporary scientific and religious explorations into the meanings of *pan-en-theos*.[6]

Just the mention of some of the schools of thought associated with it makes clear that panentheism has, to put it gently, a checkered history. And it may be that the term itself has suffered so much abuse that it is no longer useable. Nonetheless, the lines of inquiry connected with the term—combined with fresh study of biblical, patristic, and Orthodox thought—hold high promise, I believe, for a constructive response to the concerns raised by today's environmental philosophers.

I agree with Thomas Derr's conclusion: "What is historic and traditional in our valuation of creation is a perfectly sufficient guide to sound ecology. What is required of discipleship is to live out that valuation actively and faithfully." At the same time, I would add that the tradition is a living tradition; it both can and must develop, as was so masterfully explained by John Henry Newman and as has been embraced by Catholic theology under the rubric of "the development of doctrine." Here and elsewhere, I expect there are between Derr and myself differences, at least of accent, that are not unrelated to the difference between Protestant and Catholic sensibilities. Be that as it may, I am persuaded that the truth in some of the arguments that "ecophilosophers" and "ecotheologians" wrongly direct against the Christian tradition can be better grounded from within the tradition.

Here I can do no more than point to some of the directions of development that require further theological and theological-moral attention. In a colloquy on these questions, I recall being impressed by a noted Calvinist theologian who declared, "Whatever else needs to be said about the transcendence of God, we can agree that God minus the universe is still and fully God." I am not sure that I would want to flatly disagree with that formulation, but I think it is at least potentially misleading. Such an abstraction may be, to paraphrase Pascal, the God of the philosophers, but it is very doubtfully the God of Abraham, Isaac, Jacob, and God incarnate in Jesus Christ. The creation has, in Christ, been incorporated into the very Godhead—into, if one wishes to put it that way, into the very being of God.

Citing, and affirming, the wisdom of the Athenians, St. Paul declares, "In him we live and move and have our being" (Acts 17:28). And what is true of us human beings is true of all that is, the macrocosmic and microcosmic, the galaxies beyond numbering and the subatomic particles beyond discernment. In creation and redemption, God's covenantal faithfulness holds all that is, was, and ever will be to himself. In the dynamic of creation, even the millions of species that have disappeared are not finally lost. This, I believe, is the sensibility that is consonant with Jesus' words about every hair being counted and every fallen sparrow taken into Divine account. It is in this context, a context decisively shaped by God's redemptive purposes in Christ, that we can join with St. Francis of Assisi in hymns of familial and filial piety toward nature. St. Francis is, of course, a great favorite of environmentalists, but, divorced from God in Christ, such piety toward the creation becomes a form of idolatry.

The great danger is an *identification* of God and humanity, or of God and creation. God always remains other, the Ultimate Other, infinitely more than we can think or say. All our thought and language about God is analogical, and we must ever keep in mind the caution of the Fourth Lateran Council (1215) that "No similarity can be found so great but that the dissimilarity is even greater." In sharp contrast to some religious proponents of "deep ecology" who betray a monistic passion to subsume all of reality into a conceptual tapioca pudding of undifferentiated Oneness, we know that neither we nor nature is God. As our inquiries proceed analogically, they are both enriched and disciplined by an awareness of what Eastern Orthodoxy calls the "apophatic" and in Western thought is known as the *via negativa*. God is not this and God is not that, and yet this and that are not without God. All of reality is theonomous, and we do not really know the most important truth about anything, whether macrocosmic or microcosmic, until we know it, so to speak, in God.

As Derr and others note, much environmental writing is marked by a treacly sentimentality about nature, often combined, oddly enough, with a venomous contempt for the part of nature that is humanity. Such sentimentality finds expression also in patterns of Christian piety, as for instance in the popular nineteenth-century hymn "From Greenland's Icy Mountains": "What though the spicy breezes, Blow soft o'er Ceylon's isle; Though every prospect pleases, And only man is vile." The late Ernest Becker offers a bracing antidote to such nature sentimentality:

> At its most elemental level the human organism, like crawling life, has a mouth, digestive tract, and anus, a skin to keep it intact, and appendages with which to acquire food. Existence, for all organismic life, is a constant struggle to feed—a struggle to incorporate whatever other organisms they can fit into their mouths and press down their gullets without choking. Seen in these stark terms, life on this planet is a gory spectacle, a science-fiction nightmare in which digestive tracts fitted with teeth at one end are tearing away at whatever flesh they can reach, and at the other end are piling up the fuming waste excrement as they move along in search of more flesh.[7]

Such realism gives added force to our reading of St. Paul's reflection on a creation that is not yet what it will be: "We know that the whole creation has been groaning in travail together until now; and not only the creation, but we ourselves, who have the first fruits of the Spirit, groan inwardly as we wait for adoption as sons, the redemption of our bodies" (Rom. 8:22-23, RSV). The bloody horror of nature's ways, the destruction and tragedy, the manifest injustices and problems of theodicy—all these must be given full scope in any adequate Christian reflection on the world reality in which we are situated. Put differently, such a reflection must take full account of the cross in both its human and cosmic significance. As the previously cited first chapter of Colossians suggests, the peace for which we hope is through the blood of the cross.

There is much else that might be said in response to Thomas Derr's fine essay. Certainly he is right about the inescapability of humanism. Those who rail against humanism are inevitability embroiled in a task that is humanistic and even, if I may use the term, anthropocentric. They can only persuade, convince, cajole, reproach, and hope to change the minds and actions of human beings. There are no other moral agents in the universe. And those who reach to include, for example, simian cousins in the community of moral agency only underscore the unavoidably normative status of humanity. The late Abraham Joshua Heschel was fond of saying that man is the cantor and caretaker of the universe. He will only take care to the extent that, as cantor, he sings the songs that bestow meaning upon the universe and his place in it.

And so what songs should we sing in order that we might take better care? First, the song of God's sovereignty, and of our dignity derived from his caring for us. Second, the song of God's delight in his creation, of which the Bible gives many examples, and of our being invited to delight in his delight. Third, the song of reason's gift by which we understand the uses of nature to preserve and enhance the well-being of humanity—humanity being the part of creation that God became in order that we might become fully God's. Fourth, the song of Assisi, the song of fellow-feeling with all that is, and most especially with the animals of which we are forever one. Fifth, the song of wonder at a beauty that is always "other," and that, for all its brutality, bespeaks the "fearful symmetry" of Blake's abiding vision. Sixth, the song of obedience to the command to care, of faithfulness to the dominion that is delegated to us and that none other can assume. Seventh and finally, the song of redemptive hope, of the resurrection of the body; of our bodies that encompass the stuff of the creation of which we are part; of our bodies that participate in the body of Christ that is the Church, and therefore anticipate, already now, that perfect communion with God for which the whole creation waits with eager longing.

Along these lines, here only briefly sketched, we may better apprehend a creationally situated humanity, and develop an environmental theology and piety that is coherent, comprehensive, compelling, and true to the revelation of God in Christ.

Chapter 4

In Response

Thomas Sieger Derr

That the issues of environmental ethics are more than simple fodder for academic journals, that they engage vital interests everywhere, is abundantly clear from the temper of public debate. A generous sample of the passions which they elicit is on display in James Nash's spirited reply to my thesis. Our differences are many and varied, but the ones of central import center around the ascription of rights to nature. So let us begin with that, and let the rest fall into place behind it.

I have not, contrary to his complaint, ignored his "conation" argument for biotic rights, though I have not addressed it by name. After all, his book, fine as it is, is only one of the many I have consulted; and this essay is not constructed as a reply to any single one of them. I believe, however, that I really have dealt with his thesis, for it appears to be a form of the "interests" argument, which I did discuss, and reject. Interests—self-valuation, striving, desires—do not confer rights. If they did, I would be obliged to consider the interests of a mosquito in drawing my blood as a right to sustenance which I must not violate. Or if I do swat it in the act, I will have to justify my deed with reference to a calculus of conflicting and competing rights which allows some to trump others, and so on. Nash's summary solution that we should become "altruistic predators" is such a paradoxical notion that it advertises the inherent difficulty with the position it represents. Let us instead, I urge, confine "rights" to humans, find some other basis for an appropriate treatment of the natural world (as I have done), and be free of these tangles. After all, if biotic "rights" have a different basis from human rights, if they are subject to a descending scale of only partial applicability, if they do not possess equality with human rights, if they can be overridden for "the satisfaction of significant human benefits"—all of which Nash concedes—then maybe they aren't "rights" at all.

Standing behind this disagreement is our somewhat different way of interpreting the doctrines of creation and stewardship, although these variations are probably not as fundamental as they may first appear. I say very clearly that I do accept an obligation to care for the creation as a duty to its Maker. I believe I have adequately explained what I mean by this stewardship, to the point of tracing my differences with Hall and Wilkinson in the notes. I would not accept Nash's characterization of my view as treating the natural world as "nothing more than a resource base for human wants and needs." He has been led astray by misreading as a "simple assertion [which] sums up [Derr's] theology of nature," this sentence: "Nature is made for us, as we are made for God." In fact this sentence (p. 24 above) occurs in a passage describing an *anti-Christian biocentrist* view of the effects of Christian theism. It is not the way I myself would put the relation. I have said that I trust God values his creation; but not being privy to the mind of God, I must remain modest about the details. When it comes to practice, to policy public and private, I would refrain from destruction, favor restoration, practice preservation, and in cases of conflict unapologetically give priority to human need.

I do not think we can go further than that because we cannot know God's purposes with nature. Nash in his book, and again here in summary form, has made a fine theological case for loving the creation as a whole, and I gladly give him credit for it. I become uneasy when he asks that we "image the love of Christ toward all God's beloved," which means "every lifeform with which humanity is united in interdependence." We had better think carefully about microbes and cancer cells and the problem of theodicy before we say that. I am not obliged to love the leukemia which killed my sisters and my father when I was a child. I could not agree more completely with St. Paul, that we know the entire creation sighs and throbs with pain (Rom. 8:22). Loving every life form is not a solution to the problem of evil. Here again I would be inclined to genuine modesty in saying what we can know, and concentrate on making human life possible. I do not say or believe, contra Nash's reading of my essay, that "God's purposes are strictly anthropocentric." I say that we don't know, can't know, and had better not claim that we know, those purposes. Now we know only in part, said St. Paul (1 Cor. 13:12), and part of what we are permitted to know is that God cares for us.

Nash reaffirms a sentence he wrote earlier to the effect that as we humans are but latecomers and minor actors in the cosmic drama, we can have no special claim to privilege, not even in God's sight. This is a "naturalistic" statement, an inference from the natural sciences. I am not sure that Christian faith will allow such a radical discounting of the human presence, especially not if this conclusion is presented, as it is in Nash's statement, as the consequence of scientific thought. We need to remember that Christian hope is of another order entirely. Elsewhere Nash accepts a hope which actually defies natural science, going to the other extreme, as it were. He accepts the tradition of "cosmic redemption" which holds that "all life will participate in God's New Creation," which is why we must value all life now. Evidently he and I do not agree on where we will credit the authority of the natural sciences and where, in the name of Christian hope, we dare to say more. I will accept the scientific account of the likely end of the earth, and dare, by faith, to hope for a trans-natural redemption about which I am allowed to know very little save that it awaits us.

Nash obviously finds more value in the animal rights and eco-feminist movements than I do. They both claim a place in this debate, but I think they are distractions from a sober environmentalism, doing more harm than good. The animal rights movement is deeply individualistic in its ethic and has nothing to say about the questions of species or ecosystems. It is, as we have seen, hostile to an ethic which locates value in the life process as a whole ("biocentric" in common usage, though Nash wants me to follow a more recent distinction which uses "biocentric" for individualistic valuation of all life forms, and "ecocentric" for systemic valuation—an unnecessary complication for my purposes, not followed by everyone and not affecting the argument here one way or another). Nash thinks of this movement as representing one "pole"—"concern for individual life-forms"—which "must be balanced against a systemic or holistic pole for a comprehensive ecological ethic." To him these poles are "complementary;" but I think they are quite obviously in conflict, and I am hardly alone in this judgment.

As for Nash's reaction to my treatment of ecofeminism, let me say right at the start that I resist and strongly resent (there are passions on more than one side of this debate) any attempt to portray my criticism as "condescending" or "insulting" or "paternalistic." These are the dismissive words used to reject out of hand all criticism by males of anything with "feminist" in its title. I have spent virtually my entire career teaching, by choice, at a women's college, which four generations of women in my family have attended; and I have done so in the profound conviction that equality of women in society—perhaps especially in the work force—is a goal worthy of my life work. I believe that goal is diminished, demeaned, and threatened by much of what is called "ecofeminism."

I have catalogued its faults in the text and will highlight here only one important feature to which Nash objects, that the movement is infected with anti-male sexism. He says that the ecofeminist critique is directed against domineering patriarchalism, not against men as individuals or as a sex. But I have amassed more evidence to the contrary than I could use, quotation upon angry quotation attacking the way men think and *are*, by their very natures, counterpoising male *essence* to female essence. Here is the root of genuine sexism.

It may be that the ecofeminists Nash talks to all wish to remain Christians, and he has missed the rougher parts of the movement, though they are available in major anthologies. In his turn he thinks I have not duly accounted for "exceptions" to the faults I find, especially such "leading lights" as Merchant and Ruether. (Not so: see the extensive footnote citations to both.) He taxes me mightily for noting the many currents and varieties in ecofeminism, counting that as a serious methodological weakness (though elsewhere he inconsistently attacks me for *not* taking account of variations). His statement that the movement is so diverse that any attempt to criticize it is foredoomed to failure is effectively to place that movement beyond criticism. But surely no school of thought deserves such *a priori* immunity.

When his criticism comes to environmental politics, I'm afraid Nash has seriously misread me. In that section I rounded up opposing arguments on issues in environmental science, presenting them succinctly and neutrally, and then provided some methodological guidelines for sorting them out. I quite carefully did not choose sides. Against my design Nash has assigned me to one of those sides, the one he does not favor. Associating himself firmly with the "alarmists" (which is not a pejorative word in this context), he then accuses me of complacency and over-optimism. Worse yet (committing the sin of over-generalization of which he often accuses me), he has identified that side—mine, he alleges—with the political Right, which he takes as another opportunity to denounce it (and me).

142

All of this is simply wrong. I am arguing for careful appraisal of the evidence and a true willingness to listen to all sides. I cannot be assigned to one of the warring camps. It is equally mistaken to associate me with the political Right. I wish Nash would take seriously my warnings against "straight ticket" conclusions about complex science and against identifying these complicated matters *tout simple* with political parties.

Our difference here does seem to be a matter of degree, of temper perhaps. I do argue for a tilt in favor of uncertainty and danger, a hedge or margin of safety to meet outcomes worse than expected. Nash argues, if I read him right, for going further and providing for worst-case scenarios, saying that if we turn out to be wrong, we won't have lost anything serious and are likely in fact to benefit in other ways. This is a difference I am willing to let stand.

Finally, Nash taxes me repeatedly for methodological problems, so often and so insistently that one is bound to seek reasons for this drumbeat of criticism. There seems to be something really serious at issue here. He charges, again and again, that I have over-generalized, over-simplified, "caricatured," failed to take account of variations in the sub-movements described (except, curiously, ecofeminism, as noted), tarred with too wide a brush. But is the problem really the use of generalizations? I doubt it. One must construct typologies in order to have any kind of meaningful discussion, and we all do it, Nash included. I think I have been reasonably prudent in noting variations and exceptions, and I trust an attentive reader will note the many, many times I have pointed them out or otherwise qualified my judgments.

Is the problem, then, the evidence I choose to present? He does complain that my quotations are unfairly selected and not truly representative of the author cited. I believe that not to be true, and would assure him if I could that I regularly have given only a sample of the possibilities, restraining my impulse to bury such criticism under a pile of footnotes. So I doubt this is the problem either.

The problem is not really method but passionate attachment to a movement brought under sharp criticism, so that every word raised against it must seem unfair, unwarranted, the product of defective reasoning, perhaps even of ill will. Here is the making of mutual incomprehension and deadlock. But I will suggest, more hopefully, two ways to get beyond this impasse. One is Nash's accurate characterization of me, made earlier in a conference, as a reformer at heart, not one who wishes to "bash or abandon" the environmental movement, as he now charges. He was right the first time, and the first major section of my essay opens with a forthright declaration of exactly this purpose.

The second way is for him to forswear the label "biocentrist," with which I believe he has been uncomfortable, and which he may have adopted ("perhaps loosely," he admits) before he became aware of the oxymoronic potential of the term "Christian biocentrist." In fact he often doesn't seem to mean it, since he always gives priority to the human, even as he struggles with great effort to justify this preference against his alleged "biocentrism."

Returning my hope for converting *him*, one of Nash's faint hopes for *me* is that I will learn appreciation for biotic rights from my affection for my Springer spaniels. Alas, anyone who owns Springers knows that although they are sweet-tempered pets, they are also hunters who show scant regard for the "rights" or interests of smaller creatures. And to his story about the student who reconsidered biotic rights because she wouldn't needlessly kill a robin, I counterpoise this mirror-image account: A student challenged my anthropocentrism in class by saying she thought nature did have rights, the rain forest, for example. "Why?" I asked. "Because we might some day discover there new medicines to cure disease," she said. "Anthropocentric reasoning?" I suggested. And she said—yes, she really did— "Oops!"

Richard Neuhaus adds some helpful, thoughtful, and as always, gracefully phrased dimensions to my argument, and I am truly thankful for them. They extend what I have done in important places where development was needed. He and I began working on these problems at about the same time, in 1970, he in New York as the pastor of an inner-city church, I in Geneva working for the World Council of Churches. Unknown to each other, we were united in our suspicion that the nascent environmental movement did not bode well for the wretched of the earth, an accord which has clearly endured in the quarter century since.

It is also clear that our overall agreement in matters environmental is much greater than any differences, and these comments will accordingly be much briefer than those I addressed above to James Nash. Yet the differences I have with Neuhaus, slight as they are, may be both interesting and significant. Perhaps they are rooted, as he suggests, in a confessional divergence, he becoming steadily more Catholic, I remaining resolutely Protestant. And yet I think that when even this factor is taken into account, we are dealing largely in definitions and (to use a favorite Catholic word) nuance.

The central point at issue is whether I may call the humanism we share "anthropocentrism," a word which troubles him. I certainly do not mean by it that there is no transcendent Other to whom attention must be paid, nor that the ultimate ordering of our lives is not theonomous. I hope I have been clear that I hold the word within the discipline of theistic faith. I am talking rather about a focus which must be the guide for public policy. Anything else is apt to lead us badly astray, to offend against that noble humanism which both he and I wish to defend with all our moral force.

That said, I confess that Neuhaus has put his finger on the problem that indeed troubled me most in writing this book. What weight shall we give to those New Testament passages I cited (Rom. 8:18-25, Col. 1:15-20, Rev. 21:1) which seem to associate human destiny with that of the natural world? How shall we factor in the elements of the "sacred cosmos" which are undeniably present in that multiform work which is our Bible? What does it mean to speak of the transformation or "deification" of humanity, perhaps even of the earth, too?

It does not mean that either humanity or nature is divine now, of course; but does it mean that nature may become so, at least in a manner of speaking, analogous to the way we humans will be "deified"? "God became man," said Athanasius, "that man might become god." This is the Orthodox doctrine of *theosis*: the human goal is immortality, divinization, partaking of divinity. That does not mean union with the divine *essence*, however; this is not pantheism or monism. Humanity will still be distinct from God, not disappear into the deity. But there will certainly be a substantial transformation of our mortality.

Do these convictions apply also to the natural world? Importantly, because God took on flesh in the Incarnation, the doctrine of *theosis* involves the body, not the soul alone, though the full deification of the (transfigured) body must await the Last Day, the Day of Resurrection. Still, materiality is involved, which suggests that we might indeed take the next step and apply *theosis* not only to humanity, but to the material world. And Orthodoxy does take this step. The whole creation is destined for transfiguration—"cosmic redemption."

145

This is a doctrine with an honored place in Christian tradition (note Nash's appeal to it), and I respect the faith and reason of those who hold it. But when I ask myself what that really means for our treatment of the natural world, I am stumped. I have said in the text that I do not believe this concept adds anything practically to what we already know from the doctrine of creation. I do not know what more it might mean. I stick to what I think I can know with some certainty, human concerns, secure that Christian faith gives me permission to do so, as long as my vision is wide enough to encompass all humanity. My reluctance to go further, to subscribe in confidence to a full doctrine of *theosis* (at least as interpreted by the Orthodox Church) may be due in part to respect for the family and community of natural scientists in which I was raised, and even more (ah, Neuhaus is right) due to the austere Calvinist monotheism congenial to my Puritan soul.

This is an autobiographical remark, of course; but biography and theology are seldom far apart. In any case, when it comes to divinely-appointed destiny, ours or the planet's, I think it better to say too little than too much. I do not really believe the earth will be spared its final destruction when the sun expires. What will have become of the human race by then is open only to the wildest speculation. In faith I appeal once again to modesty: all creation is held in God's sight, and divine mercy will bring all to resolution. More we do not know. "Lo! I tell you a mystery," wrote St. Paul of the resurrection of the body; "The dead will be raised imperishable, and we shall be changed" (1 Cor. 15:52, RSV). And with him I rest on that hope.

Notes

Notes To Chapter 1

1. Lynn White, Jr., "The Historic Roots of Our Ecological Crisis," *Science* 155 (March 10, 1967): 1203–7.

2. George Sessions, *Environmental Philosophy: From Animal Rights to Radical Ecology*, ed. Michael Zimmerman (Englewood Cliffs, NJ: Prentice-Hall, 1993), 161 ("Introduction" to Part II).

3. Paul R. Ehrlich, *How to Be a Survivor*, with Richard L. Harriman (New York: Ballantine Books, 1971), 129.

4. White, "Continuing the Conversation," in *Western Man and Environmental Ethics: Attitudes Toward Nature and Technology*, ed. Ian G. Barbour (Reading, MA: Addison-Wesley, 1973). Also private conversations.

5. Douglas John Hall, *The Steward: A Biblical Synbol Come of Age* (Grand Rapids: Wm. B. Eerdmans, 1990); Loren Wilkinson, et al., *Earthkeeping in the Nineties: Stewardship of Creation*, revised edition (Grand Rapids: Wm. B. Eerdmans, 1991); Thomas S. Derr, *Ecology and Human Need* (Philadelphia: Westminster, 1973 and 1975). At a World Council of Churches conference at the Massachusetts Institute of Technology in 1979, the Orthodox theologian Paulos Gregorios, whose book *The Human Presence* was written largely to reply to mine, almost contemptuously dismissed the concept: "We are not likely to get very far with the idea of stewardship," he argued, in advocating his sacramental view of nature as an alternative. Yet other speakers repeatedly appealed to it, and the idea has clearly enjoyed a revival driven by the environmental movement.

6. Wilkinson, 308.

7. See my *Ecology and Human Need*, chapter 4.

8. Both also find in the model of Christ as servant a paradigm for our treatment of the natural world (Wilkinson, 12, 289–99; Hall, 120–21, 205–13, 249). But as I will make clear shortly, I believe this to be an unwarranted extension of the texts. The sacrifical servitude neither of Christ nor his followers is meant for the nonhuman world. Tellingly, all of Hall's illustrations of the principle on 249 deal with care for human beings.

9. Thus a May 1992 meeting of representatives from major religious denominations in Washington affirmed a resolution stating that the environment is a gift of God "and we must maintain it as we have received it" (reported by Jennie Moehlman, "The Religious Community

and the Environment," *Bioscience* 42, no. 8 [September 1992]: 627.) Our knowledge of natural history might give us some pause in trying to define just what the state of "original perfection" might look like.

10. See my *Ecology and Human Need*, 103–5, for a somewhat longer treatment of the relevant passages.

11. René J. Dubos, *A God Within* (New York: Scribner, 1972), 161. See 157–61 for his argument against White's thesis.

12. Clarence J. Glacken, *Traces on the Rhodian Shore: Nature and Culture in Western Thought from Ancient Times to the End of the Eighteenth Century* (Berkeley: University of California Press, 1967), 423.

13. Richard Sylvan, "Is There a Need for a New, an Environmental Ethic?" in Zimmerman, 13–14. Even Douglas John Hall, stout defender of stewardship though he is, doesn't like the "managerial approach to nature," which he all too quickly equates with wastefulness, plunder, and greed (*The Steward*, 141).

14. Paul Taylor, "The Ethics of Respect for Nature," in Zimmerman, 78–80.

15. Holmes Rolston III, *Environmental Ethics: Duties to and Values in the Natural World* (Philadelphia: Temple University Press, 1988), 9.

16. Rolston, 100.

17. Rolston, 112–16. Elsewhere ("Environmental Ethics: Some Challenges for Christians," *The Annual of the Society of Christian Ethics, 1993* [Baltimore: Georgetown University Press, 1993], 171, 184, 186), speaking to an audience of Christians, Rolston is willing to base nature's value on the doctrine of divine creation, although his goal— respecting nature's value— seems prior to the reasons for seeking it: "A forest wlderness is a sacred space. There Christians recognize God's creation, and others may find the Ultimate Reality or a Nature sacred in itself."

18. Lawrence E. Johnson, *A Morally Deep World* (Cambridge: Cambridge University Press, 1993), 6–7, 44–55, 116–17, 146, 162, 217, 287.

19. James A. Nash, *Loving Nature: Ecological Integrity and Christian Responsiblity* (Nashville: Abingdon Press, 1991), 99. See also his essay "Biotic Rights and Human Ecological Responsibilities," in *The Annual of the Society of Christian Ethics, 1993*, 137–62.

20. Rolston, *Environmental Ethics*, 218.

21. Rolston, *Environmental Ethics*, 240–41.

22. Rolston, "Environmental Ethics: Some Challenges for Christians," 179.

23. Nash, *Loving Nature*, 176, 181; "Biotic Rights," 150–51, 158–59. He would not award rights to abiotic entities, only organisms; and thus he rejects the term "rights of nature," though granting, like Rolston, that "the term remains rhetorically valuable" ("Biotic Rights," 148).

24. Rolston, *Environmental Ethics*, 48.

25. Johnson, 117–18, emphasis in the original.

26. Johnson, 185, 198.

27. Johnson, 200. See also 172–73, 243, 261, 279.

28. Rolston, *Environmental Ethics*, 50–51.

29. Larry Rasmussen's phrase, defending the extension of neighbor love even to inorganic nature; in Wesley Granberg-Michaelson, ed., *Tending the Garden: Essays on the Gospel and the Earth* (Grand Rapids: Wm. B. Eerdmans, 1987), 199. For an anti-theological version of the extension argument, see J. Baird Callicott (following his hero, the much-cited Aldo Leopold) *In Defense of the Land Ethic* (Albany: SUNY Press, 1989), 80–82.

30. H. Paul Santmire, *The Travail of Nature: The Ambiguous Ecological Promise of Christian Theology* (Philadelphia: Fortress, 1985); Nash, *Loving Nature*, 124–33.

31. Arne Naess, "The Deep Ecological Movement: Some Philosophical Aspects," in Zimmerman, 203. George Sessions is less severe but, as a "biocentric egalitarian," will give us no more than equality with nature: Nonhuman entities have "equal inherent value or worth along with humans" ("Deep Ecology and Global Ecosystem Protection," in Zimmerman, 236). Douglas John Hall urges an "openness to the mystery of all created life, including the willingness to undertake sometimes the sacrifice of our human well-being for the sake of the extra-human" (*The Steward*, 143).

32. Paul Shepard, *The Tender Carnivore and the Sacred Game* (New York: Scribner's, 1973), 269–78.

33. Rolston, *Environmental Ethics*, 155. That is not, strictly speaking, quite true. Nature has a way of restoring devastated land, whether it be laid waste by a volcano or an atomic bomb test. Extinction of species on a grand scale is not just a possibility of human activity, but is the way of nature, and always has been, well before human life appeared.

34. Richard Watson, "A Critique of Anti-Anthropocentric Biocentrism," *Environmental Ethics* 5 (1983): 252–56.

35. Roger Carras, "Are We Right in Demanding an End to Animal Cruelty?" in *On the Fifth Day: Animal Rights and Human Ethics*, ed. Richard Knowles Morris and Michael W. Fox (Washington: Acropolis Books, 1978), 136; Richard Ryder, "Experiments on Animals," in *Animals, Men, and Morals*, ed. Stanely and Rosalind Godlovitch and John Harris (New York: Taplinger, 1972), 74; Henry S. Salt, *Animals' Rights—Considered in Relation to Social Progress* (Clarks Summit, PA: Society for Animal Rights, 1980 [originally published 1892]), 94; cf. Peter Singer, *Animal Liberation* (New York: New York Review of Books, 1975), 81–82, comparing experiments on animals to experiments by Nazi doctors on "lesser" human beings; Stephen R. L. Clark, *The Moral Status of Animals* (Oxford: Oxford University Press, 1977), 66.

36. Singer, Animal Liberation, 18, 21; cf. Singer, "All Animals Are Equal," in *Animal Rights and Human Obligations*, ed. Tom Regan and Peter Singer (Englewood Cliffs, N.J.: Prentice-Hall, 1976), 154.

37. Cartesian dualism is discussed in Robert S. Brumbaugh, "Of Men, Animals, and Morals," in Morris and Fox, 14–17; see also the selection from Descartes in Andrew Linzey and Tom Regan, eds., *Animals and Christianity* (New York: Crossroad, 1988), 45–52. Charles Hartshorne, "Foundations for a Humane Ethics: What Human Beings Have in Com-

mon with Other Higher Animals," in Morris and Fox, 160. A lot of ink has been spilt, wastefully I think, over the significance of the chimpanzee language experiments, which have fascinated the animal rights movement. Steven Pinker has recently effectively dismissed them in *The Language Instinct* (New York: Morrow, 1994). For another argument against their use to prop up animal rights, see R. G. Frey, *Interests and Rights: The Case Against Animals* (Oxford: Clarendon Press, 1980), 91–100, 199–210.

38. Andrew N. Rowan, *Of Mice, Models, and Men: A Critical Evaluation of Animal Research* (Albany: SUNY Press, 1984), 88–90.

39. Michael W. Fox, "Man and Nature: Biological Perspectives," Morris and Fox, 122–23; Clark, 98ff., 104, 112; Tom Regan, *All That Dwell Therein: Animal Rights and Environmental Ethics* (Berkely: University of California Press, 1982), 13.

40. Regan, 8.

41. See, for example, John Hick, "Explaining Animal Pain," in Linzey and Regan, 63–64.

42. Joel Feinberg, "Human Duties and Animal Rights," in Morris and Fox, 60; Regan, 90, 114–15; Frey, 49.

43. Hartshorne, 155, 167.

44. Regan, 109.

45. Singer, *Animal Liberation*, 185–88.

46. Feinberg, 60, 63; John B. Cobb, Jr., "Beyond Anthropocentrism in Ethics and Religion," in Morris and Fox, 142–52.

47. Clark, 88–93, 154, 169.

48. Albert Schweitzer, "The Ethic of Reverence for Life," an excerpt from *Civilzation and Ethics* in Linzey and Regan, 118–20.

49. Regan, 169–70; Feinberg, 55–56; Singer, *Animal Liberation*, 215–16, 262–63.

50. Mark Sagoff, "Animal Liberation and Environmental Ethics: Bad Marriage, Quick Divorce," in *Environmental Philosophy: From Animal Rights to Radical Ecology*, ed. Michael E. Zimmerman (Englewood Cliffs, NJ: Prentice-Hall, 1993), 89–92.

51. Tom Regan, *The Case for Animal Rights* (Berkely: University of California Press, 1983), 262; Rolston, "Environmental Ethics: Some Challenges for Christians," 167, 173–74; Sagoff, 89.

52. Johnson, *A Morally Deep World*, 31, 74, 79–81, 126, 136–37, 153–55, 158, 162, 164, 169.

53. Johnson (64–72) does think that animals can act morally and consequently can be blamed for acting immorally. But he admits we don't know very much about animal awareness and motivation, which is, I should think, a good reason for keeping moral references out of the animal world.

54. Regan seems to know the weakness of the inherent value argument, for he admits that he cannot say what makes something inherently good or how we would know it if it were (*All That Dwell Therein*, 175–82). The concept "inherent value" seems to lack any meaning.

NOTES TO PAGES 46–53

55. James Rachels, "Do Animals Have a Right to Liberty?" in Regan and Singer, 220–21.

56. Environmental groups like Greenpeace have criticzed the subsistence whale hunting of the Intuit ("Eskimos"), but reluctantly tolerated it. Preserving the culture of tribal peoples is a popular goal among environmentalists, even if they do use rifles and outboard motors. But it is hard to see why these people should be allowed to hunt whales of plentiful species for a living and the Icelanders, for example, are not. Could it be because the latter are Europeans, not sufficiently colorful and "native"?

57. Rosemary Radford Ruether, *Gaia and God: An Ecofeminist Theology of Earth Healing* (San Francisco: Harper, 1992), 2; Carolyn Merchant, *The Death of Nature: Women, Ecology, and the Scientific Revolution* (San Francisco: Harper, 1990), xxi; cf. Ariel Salleh, "Working with Nature: Reciprocity or Control?" in Zimmerman, *Environmental Philosophy*, 313; Ynestra King, "The Ecology of Feminism and the Feminism of Ecology," in *Healing the Wounds: The Promise of Ecofeminism*, ed. Judith Plant (Philadelphia and Santa Cruz: New Society Publishers, 1989), 18; Karen Warren, "The Power and the Promise of Ecological Feminism," in *Environmental Ethics* 12, no. 2 (Summer 1990): 132–33.

58. Sherry Ortner, "Is Female to Male as Nature Is to Culture?" in *Women, Culture, and Society*, ed. Michelle Zimbalist Rosaldo and Louise Lamphere (Stanford: Stanford University Press, 1974), 84–86. For a sharp criticism of the view that women are essentially, in their very being, closer to nature than men, a criticsm which nevertheless comes from a woman who accepts and defends other precepts of ecofeminism, see Karen J. Warren, "Feminism and Ecology: Making Connections," in *Environmental Ethics* 9, no. 1 (Spring 1987): 15. In a later article she nevertheless stresses some important natural differences between the thinking of men and women; see note 63 below.

59. Riane Eisler, "The Gaia Tradition and the Partnership Future: An Eco-feminist Manifesto," in *Reweaving the World: The Emergence of Ecofeminism*, ed. Irene Diamond and Gloria Feman Orenstein (San Francisco: Sierra Club, 1990), 33; Dorothy Dinnerstein, "Survival on Earth: The Meaning of Feminism," in Plant, 200 n.15; Elizabeth Gould Davis, *The First Sex* (Baltimore: Penguin, 1971), 68–69, cited in Marianne Ferguson, *Women and Religion* (Englewood Cliffs, NJ: Prentice-Hall, 1995), 179; Charlene Spretnak, "Toward an Ecofeminist Spirituality," in Plant, 131; Spretnak, "Ecofeminism: Our Roots and Flowering," in Diamond and Orenstein, 13–14; Ruether, *Sexism and God-Talk: Toward a Feminist Theology* (Boston: Beacon Press, 1983), 265.

60. Mary Daly, quoted by Carol Christ, "Symbols of Goddess and God in Feminist Theology," in *The Book of the Goddess, Past and Present: An Introduction to Her Religion*, ed. Carl Olson (New York: Crossroad, 1983), 238; Judith Plant, "Toward a New World: An Introduction," in Plant, 5; introduction to part two, 49.

61. Ynestra King, "Healing the Wounds: Feminism, Ecology, and the Nature/Culture Dualism," in Diamond and Orenstein, 106.

62. Merchant, *The Death of Nature*, 169–72.

63. Ruether, "Toward an Ecological-Feminist Theology of Nature," in Plant, 148. Cf. Karen J. Warren, "Introduction," 260; Val Plumwood, "Nature, Self, and Gender: Feminism, Environmental Philosophy, and the Critique of Rationalsim," in Zimmerman, *Environmental Philosophy*, 286–87, 292, 299.

64. Sharon Doubiago, "Mama Coyote Talks to the Boys," in Plant, 41; Karen Waren, "The Power and the Promise of Ecological Feminism," 141–43; cf. Val Plumwood, "Nature, Self, and Gender," 290; Corinne Kumar D'Souza, "A New Movement, a New Hope: East Wind, West Wind, and the Wind from the South," in Plant, 35; Carolyn Merchant, *The Death of Nature*, 279; cf. Karen J. Warren, "Introduction," in Plant, 257–58.

65. Ruether, *Sexism and God-Talk*, 85; Ruether, *Gaia and God*, 258; King, "The Ecology of Feminism and the Feminism of Ecology," 24; Ruether, *Sexism and God Talk*, 87.

66. Merchant, *The Death of Nature*, 252.

67. Spretnak, "Our Roots and Flowering," 5.

68. Rita Gross, "Hindu Female Deities as a Resource for the Contemporary Rediscovery of the Goddess," in Olson, 228–29; Carol Christ, "Symbols of Goddess and God in Feminist Theology," 250.

69. C. Mackenzie Brown, "Kali, the Mad Mother," in Olson, 116.

70. Eisler, "The Gaia Tradition and the Partnership Future," 23–24, 26–28; Spretnak, "Toward an Ecofeminist Spirituality," 131.

71. Joan Bamberger, "The Myth of Matriarchy: Why Men Rule in Primitive Society," in Rosaldo and Lamphere, 263–66; Ortner, "Is Female to Male as Nature Is to Culture?", 70. Recently Marianne Ferguson, in *Women and Religion*, has attempted a complete construction of the thesis of an ancient matriarchal religion. It appears, however, to be such a tendentious use of "evidence," that it is likely to have a hard time with serious critics.

72. King, "Healing the Wounds," 120–21. Cf. Ruether, *Gaia and God*, 152–55.

73. Yaakov Jerome Garb, "Perspective or Escape? Ecofeminist Musings on Contemporary Earth Imagery," in Diamond and Orenstein, 274. Loren Wilkinson makes an interesting contrary argument: There may be real value in retaining masculine terminology for God. Biblical faith makes the Creator distinct from, transcendent over, his creation, not immanent. The female imagery of earth as "mother," in encouraging goddess worship, worship of nature, immanentism, and pantheism, devalues the distinctively human. The "masculine" image of God as creating by the Word is, by contrast, a very human idea; God speaks the world into being. This is not a nature image, and shows clearly the difference between God and nature. See Wilkinson, 278–79.

74. Margot Adler, "The Juice and the Mystery," in Plant,151–54. Carol Christ, "Symbols of Goddess and God in Feminist Theology," 238, 239, 245–46. Ms. Christ has withdrawn to Crete where, for a fee, she leads

"Goddess pilgrimmages" for women only, of course, inviting them to "sense Her mysteries in the darkness of caves, pour out libations of milk and honey on Minoan altars," and so on (quotations from her brochure, from "Goddess Pilgrimmage Tours," Blacksburg, VA). Cf. Naomi Goldenberg, *Changing of the Gods* (Boston: Beacon Press, 1979), 25; cited in Marianne Ferguson, *Women and Religion*, 176: "Gods who prefer men to women and spirit to body will no longer command respect. It is likely that as we watch Christ and Yahweh tumble to the ground, we will completely outgrow the need for an external God."

75. Ruether, *Gaia and God*, 240–47.

76. Vandana Shiva, "Development, Ecology, and Women," in Plant, 81.

77. Eisler, "The Gaia Tradition and the Partnership Future," 32. Cf. Ruether, *Sexism and God-Talk*, 84–85.

78. King, "Healing the Wounds," 107.

79. Merchant, *The Death of Nature*, 294.

80. These accusations are made explicitly by Warwick Fox, for example, in "The Deep Ecology-Ecofeminism Debate and Its Parallels," in *Environmental Ethics* 11, no. 1 (Spring 1989): 16–18. Fox is, however, defending deep ecology's anti-anthropocentrism, which is obviously contrary to my purpose here.

81. Ruether, *Sexism and God-Talk*, 91–92.

82. For a quick sampling of serious and responsible works on both sides of the ledger, from which the following statisics have been culled, see, for the alarmists, Lester R. Brown, *State of the World, 1984* [and subsequent years] (Washington: Worldwatch Institute, 1984–1995); Albert Gore, *Earth in the Balance* (Boston: Houghton Mifflin, 1992); Rachel Carson, *Silent Spring* (Boston: Houghton Mifflin, 1962); Paul R. Ehrlich, *The Population Bomb* (New York: Ballentine, 1968) and *The Population Explosion* (New York: Touchstone, 1990); Paul Ehrlich and Anne Ehrlich, *The End of Affluence* (New York: Ballentine, 1976); Garrett Hardin, *Exploring New Ethics for Survival: The Voyage of the Spaceship Beagle* (Baltimore: Penguin, 1973); Robert L. Heilbroner, *An Inquiry into the Human Prospect* (New York: Norton, 1975, and revisions 1980, 1991), Bill McKibben, *The End of Nature* (New York: Random House, 1989), Donella H. Meadows et al., *The Limits to Growth* (New York: Universe Books, 1972); Lester W. Milbrath, *Envisioning a Sustainable Society: Learning Our Way Out* (Albany: SUNY Press, 1989); and, on the more cautious or even optimistic side, Ronald Bailey, *Ecoscam: The False Prophets of Ecological Apocalypse* (New York: St. Martin's, 1993); Bailey, ed., *The True State of the Planet*, (New York: The Free Press, 1995); Michael Fumento, *Science Under Siege: Balancing Technology and the Environment* (New York: William Morrow, 1993); John Royden Maddox, *The Doomsday Syndrome* (New York: McGraw Hill, 1972); Julian Simon, *The Ultimate Resource* (Princeton: Princeton University Press, 1981); Joseph L. Blast, Peter J. Hill, and Richard C. Rue, *Eco-Sanity: A Common-Sense Guide to Environmentalism* (Lanham MD: Madison Books, 1994); Charles T. Rubin, *The Green Crusade: Rethinking the*

Roots of Environmentalism (New York: The Free Press, 1994); Gregg Easterbrook, *A Moment on the Earth: The Coming Age of Environmental Optimism* (New York: Viking, 1995).

83. Anthony Weston, "Forms of Gaian Ethics," *Environmental Ethics* 9 (1987): 220.

84. Weston, "Forms of Gaian Ethics," 221. The same figure (30 million extant today out of 30 billion since the Cambrian age) is given by Richard Leakey and Roger Lewin in *The Sixth Extinction: Patterns of Life and the Future of Humankind* (New York: Doubleday 1995), cited by Paul Rabinow in the *New York Times Book Review*, Nov. 12, 1995, 60.

85. Ehrlich, *The Population Bomb*, i.

86. Bailey, *Ecoscam*, 6

87. Paul Ehrlich and Anne Ehrlich, *Healing the Planet: Strategies for Resolving the Environmental Crisis* (New York: Addison-Wesley 1991), 242.

88. Including Herman E. Daly and John B. Cobb Jr., *For the Common Good: Redirecting the Economy toward Community, the Environment, and a Sustainable Future* (Boston: Beacon Press, 1989), 251, who endorse a resort to coercion if voluntary population control programs do not succeed.

89. Hardin, "The Tragedy of the Commons," *Science* 162 (1968): 378. The totalitarian thrust of environmentalism is well discussed by Charles Rubin in his essay "Managing the Planet: The Politics of 'The Environment,'" in *Creation at Risk? Religion, Science, and the Environment*, ed. Michael Cromartie (Grand Rapids: Wm. B. Eerdmans, 1995) 1–16, although he is quite careful to say that the charge does not apply to all environmentalists. As far as I know, these totalitarian implications were first pointed out by Richard John Neuhaus in his brilliant polemic against environmental excess, *In Defense of People: Ecology and the Seduction of Radicalism* (New York: Macmillan, 1971), 112–13.

90. Murray Bookchin, "What Is Social Ecology?" in Zimmerman, 354–55, 365–70. Another environmentalist who rejects capitalism (as well as nationalism) out of hand is Douglas John Hall, on the grounds that because the earth's resources belong to God, they must be available for the common use, and ought not to fall into a few private hands (*The Steward*, 178).

91. Ruether, *Sexism and God-Talk*, 83; Merchant, *The Death of Nature*, 89; Ruether, *Sexism and God-Talk*, 263.

92. Bookchin, 362

93. Judith Plant, "The Circle is Gathering. . . ." in Plant, 249; "Consensus and Community: An Interview with Caroline Estes," in Plant, 240–41; Ruether, *Gaia and God*, 57–58.

94. Two of the more thorough advocates of this point of view are Daly and Cobb, *For the Common Good*; see especially 16–18, 50, 94–95, 165–75, 209–29, 283–96, 348–49. They call their position neither capitalist nor socialist, but a "third way" which favors a regulated market economy where individual choices are limited "for the common good." Third way or no, the book definitely belongs to the genre of ecological crisis screed.

95. For a good example of this approach to environmental improve-

ment see William J. Baumol and Wallace E. Oates, *Economics, Environmental Policy, and the Quality of Life* (Englewood Cliffs, NJ: Prentice-Hall, 1979), especially 114–15, 165–72, 231–44, 250–78, 307–13, 323–41, 367–69.

96. For a wholly adulatory report on this fringe element see Christopher Manes, *Green Rage: Radical Environmentalism and the Unmaking of Civilization* (Boston: Little, Brown, 1990). "Earth First!" has since come unravelled, perhaps what one ought to expect of a movement operating outside the law.

97. Wilkinson, 244–46. Cf. Mark Sagoff, *The Economy of the Earth* (Cambridge, Cambridge University Press, 1988).

98. Wilkinson, 251.

99. Baumol and Oates, 283–91. Wilkinson and colleagues suggest that if we start with scarcity and property rights, and are paying for what we take, we will economize out of self-interest. But if we start with the stewardship approach, we will economize in our use of things because we are responsible for creation (*Earthkeeping* 241). They appear to be more optimistic about the selfless motive than Baumol and Oates.

100. When I wrote *Ecology and Human Need* twenty-five years ago, there was virtually nothing available on responsibility to future generations. Chapter 5 of that book, "The Obligation to the Future," was thus pretty much an exercise in pure thought, devoid of references. Since then the subject has become a regular topic in environmental ethics, including Ernest Partridge, ed., *Responsibilities to Future Generations* (Buffalo: Prometheus Books, 1981), which includes my chapter (37–44). The argument which follows here is a much-condensed version of that essay, with some alterations and a second thought or two.

101. Gen. 13:15; cf. 9:9; 17:7-19; 23:17-18; 26:3-5; 28:13-14; 35:12; Exod. 33:1; Deut. 7:9.

102. See the fine criticism of the ethical implications of bioregionalism in Rubin, *The Green Crusade*, 200–203.

103. This is the general view of the U.N.'s World Commission on Environment and Development in its report *Our Common Future* (Oxford: Oxford University Press, 1987), 46. The report believes in natural limits to development and in egalitarian redistribution of wealth.

104. This is the position of Loren Wilkinson and colleagues in *Earthkeeping*: "We can no longer assume that 'environment' and 'development' have conflicting agendas" (352; cf. 358).

105. One of my students, Darcy M. Goddard, in a carefully researched study done for one of my courses, "Environmental Ethics and Third World Development: Striking an Ethical Balance," comes to this conclusion, and persuades me that she is right.

106. Something like this did happen at a 1974 meeting of the World Council of Churches' Working Committee on Church and Society where a sharp disagreement on the future of the program pitted the development and justice concerns of "third world" representatives against westerners who wanted an environmental emphasis. I slipped a note to Paul Abrecht, the executive secretary, suggesting that to avoid a standoff the

new program should be called "the just and sustainable society." And in short order that is exactly what happened—not because there was a logical connection, but because both sides had to be satisifed. Through a couple of metamorphoses and considerable expansion the program has subsequently become the current "Justice, Peace, and the Integrity of Creation."

107. Hardin, *Exploring New Ethics for Survival*, passim.

108. Vandana Shiva, "Development as a New Project of Western Patriarchy," in Diamond and Orenstein, 193; "Joint Appeal by Religion and Science for the Environment," a project of a mixed group including astronomer Carl Sagan, then-senator Albert Gore, and James Parks Morton, Dean of the Cathedral of St. John the Divine in New York, printed in *BioScience* 42, no. 8 (September 1992): 624–25.

109. Wilkinson, 330, 336–38. They acknowledge that this is a rather "broad" picture of justice.

110. Ruether, *Sexism and God-Talk*, 91.

111. Clark, *The Moral Status of Animals*, 7, 8, 42 n. 7, 77, 148, 171 n. 8; Ruether, *Sexism and God-Talk*, 88; Taylor, "The Ethics of Respect for Nature," 71, 81; Taylor, "In Defense of Biocentrism," 238; Berry, "The Viable Human," in Zimmerman, 174; Wilson, "Is Humanity Suicidal?" *The New York Times Magazine*, 30 May 1993, 24. Wilson does make it clear that he wants to preserve the natural world for human benefit and so avoid our disappearance, but there is an anti-humanistic force to his statements nonetheless.

112. Rolston, *Environmental Ethics*, 103.

113. Hardin's essay, "The Tragedy of the Commons," *Science* 162 (December 1968), is still routinely cited and anthologized, as is the conclusions he drew from it in another essay, "Living on a Lifeboat," *Bioscience* 24 (1974). But harshest of all is the essay's expansion in *Exploring New Ethics for Survival*, which is virtually invisible today. The quotation from Aiken is from an essay "Ethical Issues in Agriculture," in *Earthbound: New Introductory Essays in Environmental Ethics*, ed. Tom Regan (New York: Random House, 1984), 269; cited in Callicott, 92. This is not Aiken's position, though Callicott's alterations make it appear to be so. Aiken says that these statements, which in his essay are questions, would be those of a position he calls "eco-holism," an extreme stance which he suggests may be ascribed to Paul Taylor among others, and which he rejects in favor of a more humanistic one. On p. 272 he outlines a scale of comparative value much like Nash's, one which favors humans.

114. White, "The Future of Compassion," *The Ecumenical Review* 30, no. 2 (April 1978): 108. Had he lived, he would perhaps have seen AIDS as the fulfillment of his unvoiced prayer.

115. Rolston, *Environmental Ethics*, 329; Rolston, "Challenges in Environmental Ethics," in Zimmerman, 136; Nash, "Biotic Rights," 159; Callicott, 93–94; Wilkinson, 295; Johnson, 7–8, 243, 258; Taylor, "In Defense of Biocentrism," *Environmental Ethics* 5 (1983): 242–243. The dangers in confounding and confusing the ethical treatment of people and the

natural world are unwittingly illustrated by Wilkinson and colleagues who, in a catalogue of "humanity's destructive sinfulness" list, side by side, "Nazis cremating millions of Jews, Americans slaughtering billions of passenger pigeons, . . ." (14)—an example of the moral equivalence theory gone wildly awry.

116. Christ, "Rethinking Theology and Nature," in Diamond and Orenstein, 68.

117. Rolston, *Environmental Ethics*, 185–186, 195–198, 344–345, quoting (in part) P. C. W. Davies.

118. James A. Gustafson, *A Sense of the Divine: The Natural Environment from a Theocentric Perspective* (Cleveland: Pilgrim Press, 1995), 47, 103; Nash, 233–34, n. 10, commenting on the first volume of Gustafson's *Ethics from a Theocentric Perspective*, 2 vols. (Chicago: University of Chicago, 1981), 1:106, 183–84, 248–50, 270–73.

119. Michael Zimmerman, "Deep Ecology and Ecofeminism: The Emerging Dialogue," in Diamond and Orenstein, 140. Zimmerman, like Naess and Sessions, is a "biocentric egalitarian," thus: "Humanity is no more, but also no less, important than all other things on earth" (ibid.).

120. Norton, "Environmental Ethics and Weak Anthropocentrism," *Environmental Ethics* 6 (Summer 1984): 134–36. "Wise use," while an intellectually obvious and easily defensible concept from an anthropocentric point of view, has also been misappropriated by those who would use it to defeat all efforts at conservation. The term must be read carefully in context to discern its real intent.

121. Bertrand Russell, *A Free Man's Worship* (Portland, ME: Thomas Mosher, 1927), 6, 7, 27.

122. Heilbroner, *An Inquiry into the Human Prospect*, 13, 22.

123. William Faulkner, "Upon Receiving the Nobel Prize for Literature, 1950," in *Essays, Speeches and Public Letters by William Faulkner*, ed. James B. Meriweather (New York: Random House, 1965), 120.

124. Ps. 71:5, 33:18; Rom. 5:2, 5; 1 Cor. 13:13; 1 Tim. 4:10; Col. 1:23; 1 Pet. 3:15.

Notes to Chapter 2

1. James A. Nash, *Loving Nature: Ecological Integrity and Christian Responsibility* (Nashville: Abingdon Press, 1991).

2. See Richard John Neuhaus, *In Defense of People: Ecology and the Seduction of Radicalism* (New York: Macmillan, 1971), a book which Derr describes as a "brilliant polemic against environmental excess" and which provides a model for his project.

3. See *Loving Nature*, chapter 3.

4. Several of these sections are revised versions of material that originally appeared in *Creation at Risk? Religion, Science, and Environmentalism*, ed. Michael J. Cromartie (Grand Rapids: Wm. B. Eerdmans, 1995). I am grateful for permission to use that material here.

5. Douglas John Hall, *Imaging God: Dominion as Stewardship* (Grand Rapids: Wm. B. Eerdmans, 1986), 76–87.

6. Loren Wilkinson, et al., *Earthkeeping: Christian Stewardship of Natural Resources* (Grand Rapids: Wm. B. Eerdmans, 1980), 214–16.

7. James A. Nash, "Toward the Ecological Reformation of Christianity," *Interpretation: A Journal of Bible and Theology* 50, no. 1 (January 1996): 8.

8. *Loving Nature*, 93–138.

9. Ibid., chapter 7; James A. Nash, "Biotic Rights and Human Ecological Responsibility," *The Annual of the Society of Christian Ethics 1993* 137–62; and James A. Nash, "The Case for Biotic Rights," *Yale Journal of International Law* 18, no. 11 (1993): 235–49.

10. See my "Human Rights and the Environment: New Challenge for Ethics," *Theology and Public Policy* 4, no. 2 (Fall 1992): 42–57.

11. See Heather Eaton, "Ecological-Feminist Theology: Contributions and Challenges," in *Theology for Earth Community: A Field Guide*, ed. Dieter T. Hessel (Maryknoll, N.Y.: Orbis Books, 1996), 77–92.

12. "Ecofeminism, Reverence for Life, and Feminist Theological Ethics," in *Liberating Life: Contemporary Approaches to Ecological Theology*, eds. Charles Birch, William Eakin, and Jay B. McDaniel (Maryknoll, NY: Orbis Books, 1990), 90–92.

13. Michaels makes the serious charge that the federal funding of climatological research has corrupted its scientific findings, while he denies that his own research has been biased by funding from oil and coal interests. See Patrick J. Michaels, "The Climate-Change Debacle: The Perils of Politicizing Science." *Creation at Risk? Religion, Science, and Environmentalism*, ed. Michael J. Cromartie (Washington and Grand Rapids: Ethics and Public Policy Center and Eerdmans, 1995), 51–53; Gary Lee, "Industry Funds Global-Warming Skeptics," *The Washington Post*, Thursday, March 21, 1996, p. A8.

14. For popular defenses of the Act, see, for example, Ted Williams, "Finding Safe Harbor," 26–32, and T. H. Watkins, "What's Wrong with the Endangered Species Act? Not Much and Here's Why," 37–41, *Audubon* 98, no. 1 (Jan.–Feb. 1996).

15. See my "Moral Values in Risk Decisions," in *Handbook for Environmental Risk Decision Making: Values, Perceptions and Ethics*, ed. C. Richard Cothern (Boca Raton, FL: CRC Press/Lewis Publishers, 1996), 199– 200.

16. See *Agenda 21: The UN Programme of Action from Rio* (New York: United Nations Publications, 1992). Cf. World Commission on Environment and Development, *Our Common Future* (New York: Oxford University Press, 1982).

17. World Resources Institute in collaboration with the UN Environment Programme and the UN Development Programme, *World Resources 1994–95* (New York: Oxford University Press, 1994), 338–39 (table 21.4).

18. Bread for the World Institute, *Hunger 1995: Causes of Hunger* (Silver Spring, MD: BFWI, 1994), 62, 65–66.

19. Sandra Postel, "Carrying Capacity: Earth's Bottom Line," *State of*

the World, 1994: A Worldwatch Institute Report on Progress Toward a Sustainable Society (New York: W. W. Norton, 1994), 10.

20. Lester Brown, "Facing Food Insecurity," *State of the World, 1994,* 179–87.

21. Mark Hertsgaard, "Who's Afraid of Global Warming? Surprise! It's Big Business That's Worried Now," *The Washington Post* (Sunday, January 27, 1996).

22. On ecojustice, see especially *After Nature's Revolt: Eco-Justice and Theology,* ed. Dieter T. Hessel (Minneapolis: Fortress Press, 1992), and *Ecology, Justice, and Christian Faith: A Guide to the Literature, 1960–93,* compiled by Peter W. Bakken, J. Ronald Engel, and Joan Gibb Engel (Westport, CT.: Greenwood Press, 1995).

Notes to Chapter 3

1. Richard John Neuhaus, *In Defense of People: Ecology and the Seduction of Radicalism* (New York: Macmillan, 1971).

2. See above, p. 92.

3. Caroline Walker Bynum, *The Resurrecxtion of the Body in Western Christianity* (New York: Columbia University Press, 1995).

4. Benedict Ashley, O.P., *Theologies of the Body: Humanist and Christian* (Braintree, Mass.: Pope John Center, 1985), 695.

5. Von Balthasar's reflections are, as usual, spread throughout his enormous oeuvre, but see *The Glory of the Lord,* Volume 5: *A Theological Aesthetics,* translated by Erasmo Leiva-Merikakis, edited by Joseph Fessio S.J. and John Riches (San Francisco: Ignatius Press, and New York: Crossroad Publications, 1991), 525ff.

6. Wolfhart Pannenberg, *Systematic Theology,* Volume 2, translated by Geoffrey W. Bromiley (Grand Rapids: Wm. B. Eerdmans, 1994).

7. Ernest Becker, *Escape From Evil* (New York: The Free Press, 1975), 1.

Contributors

Thomas Sieger Derr is Professor of Religion at Smith College. Previously on the staff of the World Council of Churches, he was a participant in the 1979 Conference on "Faith, Science and the Future" hosted by M.I.T. His many writings include *Ecology and Human Need* (1975) and *Barriers to Ecumenism: The Holy See and the World Council on Social Questions* (1983).

James A. Nash, who served for many years as head of the Massachusetts Council of Churches, is currently the Executive Director of the Churches' Center for Theology and Public Policy, and editor of its journal, *Theology and Public Policy*. His most recent book is *Loving Nature: Ecological Integrity and Christian Responsibility* (1991).

Richard John Neuhaus is the Director of the Institute on Religion and Society, and editor of the journal, *First Things*. Known for his activism in several areas, he is also author of a number of books, including *In Defense of People: Ecology and the Seduction of Radicalism* (1971), and *The Naked Public Square* (1984).

Max L. Stackhouse is Professor of Christian Ethics at Princeton Theological Seminary. He is the primary editor of *On Moral Business: Classical and Contemporary Resources for Ethics and Economic Life* (1995), and author of *Public Theology and Political Economy* (1986, 1991) and *Creeds, Society and Human Rights* (1984).